Myths and H
of Caribbean I

CARIBBEAN ARCHAEOLOGY AND ETHNOHISTORY

Series Editor Antonio L. Curet

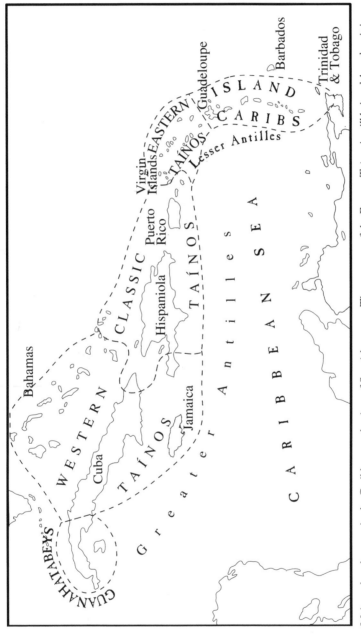

Major cultural groups in the Caribbean at the time of Spanish contact. The presence of the Eastern Taínos is still being debated, as it is unclear whether the Northern Antilles was in fact Taíno or Taíno-influenced because of trade interactions between the natives of this area and the Taínos of Hispaniola and Puerto Rico. (Adapted from Rouse, *The Taínos*. Used with permission.)

Myths and Realities of Caribbean History

Basil A. Reid

THE UNIVERSITY OF ALABAMA PRESS
Tuscaloosa

Typeface Caslon

Library of Congress Cataloging-in-Publication Data

Reid, Basil A., 1961–
    Myths and realities of Caribbean history / Basil A. Reid.
        p.   cm. — (Caribbean archaeology and ethnohistory)
    Includes bibliographical references and index.
    ISBN 978-0-8173-5534-0 (pbk. : alk. paper) 1. Caribbean Area—History—Errors,
inventions, etc. I. Title.
    F2176.R43 2009
    972.9′01—dc22

                                                        2008035776

    ISBN 978-0-8173-8316-9 (electronic)

Contents

Illustrations

Foreword

History is alive! It is a subject that is continuously adding new information, new interpretations, and new perspectives on the past. It has also been used to serve political, cultural, and social objectives to the point where many historical treatises are best described as propaganda. Nowhere is this more apparent than in the colonialist efforts to portray the grand heritage of the colonizers and to deny any history to the peoples they subjugated. Historian Michael Craton expressed this quite eloquently in his study of enslaved peoples in Jamaica, titled *Searching for the Invisible Man.*

History operates on several levels. At its most abstract, historians debate the roles of methods and theories for creating the past. Debates concerning the interpretation of particular events and historical processes comprise a second level in which different interpretations of the "facts" compete for acceptance and seek to represent different perspectives on the past. It is through these filters that popular histories are constructed. This end product often has been presented as the story of great men, their extraordinary deeds, and the times in which these deeds were accomplished.

For the masses, formal history is dead. It is little more than a random collection of names and dates. You memorize the facts, take and pass your exams, and then forget everything you learned because it has no relevance in your life. Although this is an easy way to progress toward a diploma and profession, you sacrifice your soul in doing so. As Bob Marley sang, "If you know your history, then you would know where you're coming from."

Many people are content to leave the debates concerning Caribbean history to the professionals. Unfortunately this approach excludes the general public, and their knowledge and understanding of the past are then based on outmoded notions concerning the peoples who lived in the past. But history is not simply a collection of faceless facts. It is the story of people, their ancestors, the chaos of their daily lives, and of how all of us developed and changed to reach the present. And it plays an active role in charting our futures.

Fortunately, there are a few scholars who recognize the role of history and have the necessary skills to translate new developments, new ideas, and new interpretations into a language that is easily understood by the general public. Basil Reid is exceptional in this regard. Dr. Reid recognized that many popular beliefs, which he calls myths, reflect inaccurate and sometimes colonialist interpretations of the past. In this fascinating book he systematically dissects these myths and points the direction toward new interpretations and perspectives. In doing so he enriches all of our lives by improving our understanding of the past.

William F. Keegan
Curator of Caribbean Archaeology at the Florida
Museum of Natural History and Professor of Anthropology and Latin American Studies at the University
of Florida, Gainesville

Introduction

This book seeks to correct many of our misconceptions about precolonial and European-contact periods in the Caribbean. It is also intended to inform popular audiences as well as scholars about the current state of archaeological/historical research in the Caribbean and the value of this research in fostering a better understanding of the region's past. History is based not only on written records but also on a rich array of archaeological and oral data. Contrary to popular opinion, the history of the Caribbean did not begin with the arrival of the Europeans in 1492. It started about seven thousand years earlier with the advent of Archaic groups from South America, then the migration of other Archaic groups from Central America about two thousand years thereafter. The next wave of migrants, the Saladoids, came from South America in 500 B.C. and, like their Archaic forerunners, established several indigenous communities in the Caribbean. These communities eventually evolved into new cultural groups, creating a rich tapestry of cultural traditions and indigenous societies throughout the northern and southern Caribbean. The misuse of the terms "Arawak" and "Ciboneys," and the inaccuracy of references to Carib cannibalism are among the eleven myths debunked in this book.

Archaeological/historical research of the precolonial and contact periods is ongoing, offering new insights into our understanding of these early cultures. A prime example of this concerns which group was the first to have brought pottery-making and agriculture to the Caribbean. For years, the Arawaks were touted as the first; then the Saladoids were accorded that honor; and recently the Archaic peoples have been deemed to be the first potters and farmers. Such is the nature of the beast in academia, where open-mindedness and a willingness to debate the issues are essential as we contend with sometimes controversial subject matters in the marketplace of ideas. As new evidence emerges to disprove notions about the past, these notions should be replaced by new ones, regardless of how long they have been actively promoted in books and articles.

The sifting of the most current evidence to determine facts from myths is this book's primary purpose.

I acknowledge the generous assistance of Naseema Hosein-Hoey, who typed and collated some of the research materials and helped prepare the glossary, and Christopher Riley, who produced most of the visual materials. I also gratefully acknowledge the copyright permissions given by Yale University Press, the University of Alabama Press, Princeton University Press, University Press of Florida, Wellcome Trustees, the Crow Canyon Archaeological Center, Arie Boomert, David Watters, Anne Stokes, David Steadman, Jay B. Haviser, Philip Allsworth-Jones, Michiel Kappers, Richard Callaghan, Marc Dorst, José Oliver, Paul Comeau, Yasmin Baksh-Comeau, Reg. Murphy, and Peter L. Drewett. I am very grateful to both William Keegan and Luis Antonio Curet for reviewing the text and providing constructive criticism. I also thank William Keegan for writing the foreword.

Finally, I profusely thank my beloved wife, Joan, and our son, Gavin, for their incredible patience and generous moral support, as I spent time drafting, writing, rewriting, and editing the book. This book is dedicated to these two fine individuals.

Myth 1

Caribbean History Started with the Arrival of Christopher Columbus in 1492

History is often associated with the introduction of writing. But the people who lived in the Caribbean before Columbus arrived had a rich and well-rehearsed oral history, and left a record of their activities that can be studied using archaeological methods.

~

Definitions of History

History is not based only on written records but on all human actions, including those recorded orally and reflected exclusively in the archaeological record. The conventional definition of history says that Caribbean history began with the arrival of Christopher Columbus in the Caribbean in 1492 (Figure 1.1). However, all events relating to nonliterate societies, whether before or after European contact, are historical by definition. Early European societies were generally considered literate, even though many of those who traveled to the Caribbean in search of gold were probably unable to read and write. With the arrival of the early Europeans came writing and the use of written records to document the events of the day. As no tangible evidence for pre-colonial Amerindian writing has been found in the Caribbean, it has been argued that the native peoples of the region were totally devoid of a history until the arrival of Christopher Columbus.

According to Eurocentric beliefs, nonliterate peoples did not really have a history, a view reflected in Lévi-Strauss's well-known distinction between rapidly transforming "hot" societies with a history on the one hand, and slow-moving "cold" societies without a history on the other. Implicit in this approach is the assumption that colonial contacts produced the first drastic cultural or historical changes in these cold societies, which presumably had peaceful and unchanging cultures during the preceding millennia. Studying pre-Columbian

Figure 1.1. *An Indian Cacique of the Island of Cuba, Addressing Columbus Concerning a Future State.* (From Bryan Edwards, *The History, Civil and Commercial, of the British Colonies in the West Indies* [London, 1819].)

societies in the ethnographic present also portrays them as timeless primitives completely devoid of a history until the arrival of the early Europeans.

The English word *prehistory* was first introduced in 1851 by Daniel Wilson in the title of his book *The Prehistoric Annals of Scotland* (Darvill 2002). The French *préhistorique* has been used since the 1830s to refer to the time before the appearance of writing (Darvill 2002). In the archaeological literature, the precolonial peoples of the New World are routinely labeled as prehistoric, with "prehistoric" generally referring to the time before written history (Darvill 2002). However, the dichotomy of prehistory versus history is really a product of Western linear time conception and is therefore not entirely applicable to a study of native societies in the Caribbean. Hastrup (1992) correctly argued

1498	Columbus lands on Trinidad.
1592	San José de Oruña (now St. Joseph) founded in Trinidad.
1783	A *cédula de población* (land grant) declared by Spain.
1797	Trinidad captured by the British.
1888	Trinidad and Tobago incorporated into a single Crown colony.
1962	Trinidad and Tobago gains political independence from Great Britain.
1976	Trinidad and Tobago becomes a republic.

Figure 1.2. A time line for Trinidad and Tobago from the time of Western contact.

that the Western views of the past and of time are clearly different from ancient or non-Western societies, but are in no way superior to them.

Linear Time

Westerners think of the passage of the human experience along a straight, if branching, highway of time. The great nineteenth-century German statesman Otto von Bismarck called this the "stream of time," upon which all human societies ride for a time (Fagan 2002). We have a sense of linear, unraveling history that goes back through approximately five hundred years of recorded history in Trinidad and Tobago. For example, students of Trinidad and Tobago's history would be familiar with the milestones shown in Figure 1.2. These were are all important landmarks along the ladder of Trinidad and Tobago's historical chronology, which continues to unfold daily as people live their lives in the twin island republic (Fagan 2002). For decades, an unfolding, linear past defined our perception of history. Therefore, the Amerindians of Trinidad and Tobago, whose past is largely undocumented and whose time conception was predominantly cyclical, are usually perceived as completely lacking in histories of their own, even though their past extended as far back as seven thousand years ago.

Eurocentric Concept of History Challenged

Since the 1980s and 1990s, this Eurocentric concept of history has been increasingly challenged (Gell 1996; Gosden 1994; Schmidt 1997; Schmidt and Patterson 1996; Wolf 1982). Wolf (1982) makes it clear that European expansion on a global scale, which began around 1400, encountered human societies and cultures characterized by "long and complex histories." He further challenges those who think that Europeans were the only ones who made history (Wolf 1982). History is increasingly being redefined as not restricted to written records but to the dating of events, whether orally or in writing. In short, there is growing recognition among researchers that past non-Western, non-literate societies, including pre-Columbian societies in the Caribbean, had dynamic histories.

While the world-system theory of Immanuel Wallerstein (2004) suggests that non-Western societies (referred to as the "periphery" in Wallerstein's model) are inherently static and timeless, the reality is that the so-called periphery was culturally diverse, variable in its forms, and dynamic. In essence, the world-system theory is unable to account for the diversity of local responses to the world-system (Sahlins 1987) within the periphery such as anti-imperialist activities, labor strikes, and the creation of indigenous cultural expressions (Buckridge 2004). Given that many colonial peoples managed to successfully throw off the yoke of European political subjugation through militant action and protracted warfare tells us that the so-called periphery was far from being either static or timeless (Rush 1999).

The tendency by scholars to present the concepts of *history* and *time* as one and the same is reflective of the increasingly prevalent reconceptualization of history. All human actions produce time and every human act constitutes an event or part of a succession of events (Gosden 1994). Also referred to as history (Munn 1992), time is based on dated events (Gell 1996) and dated events do not necessarily relate to calendars or European timepieces such as clocks and watches. They can also be based on seasons, and on annual festivals coupled with the birth and death of important persons in communities. For instance in the 1930s, Evans-Pritchard observed that the time conception of the Nuer of Sudan in north Africa revolved around dates linked to their wet and dry seasons, group social activities (ecological time-reckoning), and Nuer relations to one another in respect to age and kinship ties (structural time-reckoning) (Evans-Pritchard 1939) (Figure 1.3). For more contemporary groups, such as the Luo people of western Kenya, time, or history, is also cyclical, comprising a host of temporal measures involving life, generational, and ritual cycles. The Bali calendar is to some extent not a scheme of time measurement but rather a component of a cyclical system of action. Essentially, this system revolves around ritual observances (such as temple festivals, which occur sporadically throughout the year), personal actions dictated by the conjunction of personal days (birthdays, auspicious days, etc.), and days recognized as being good for particular activities, such as getting married, making a start on an important project, and so on (Gell 1996).

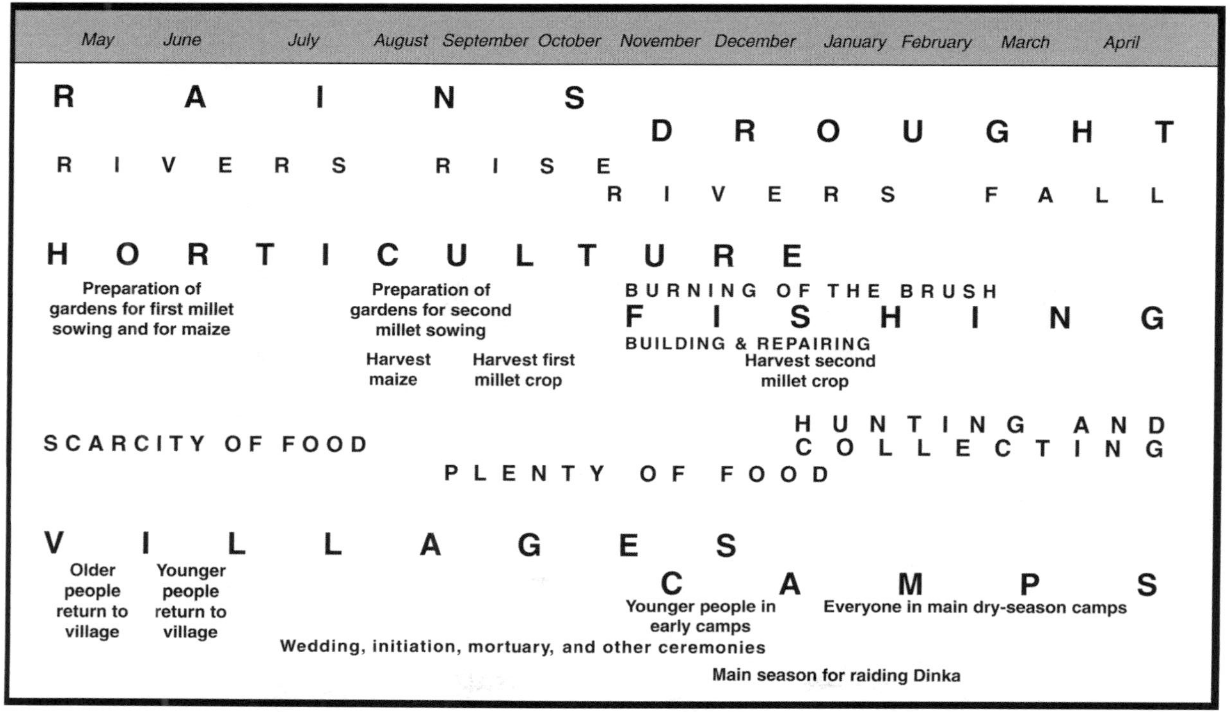

May	June	July	August	September	October	November	December	January	February	March	April
R	A	I	N	S	D	R	O	U	G	H	T
	R	I	V	E	R	S	R	I	S	E	
					R	I	V	E	R	S	F A L L

H O R T I C U L T U R E

- Preparation of gardens for first millet sowing and for maize
- Preparation of gardens for second millet sowing
- Harvest maize
- Harvest first millet crop
- BURNING OF THE BRUSH
- BUILDING & REPAIRING — Harvest second millet crop
- F I S H I N G

SCARCITY OF FOOD | PLENTY OF FOOD

H U N T I N G A N D C O L L E C T I N G

V I L L A G E S | C A M P S

- Older people return to village
- Younger people return to village
- Wedding, initiation, mortuary, and other ceremonies
- Younger people in early camps
- Everyone in main dry-season camps
- Main season for raiding Dinka

Figure 1.3. Nuer time-reckoning system based on seasons and social activities. (Reproduced from Evans-Pritchard, "Nuer Time-Reckoning.")

Non-Western societies do not perceive themselves as living in a change-less world; many of them make a clear distinction between the recent past, which lies within living memory, and the more remote past, which came before memory (Fagan 2002). For instance, the Australian Aboriginal groups living in northeast Queensland distinguish between *kuma*, the span of events witnessed by living people; *anthantnama*, a long time ago; and *yilamu*, the period of creation (Fagan 2002). The ancient Maya developed an elaborate cyclical calendar of interlocking secular and religious calendars to measure the passage of the seasons and to regulate religious ceremonies.

It is likely that precolonial peoples of the Caribbean used techniques similar to those of the early Hawaiians of the Pacific (Sahlins 1987) and the Nuer people of Sudan of Africa (Evans-Pritchard 1939) to measure or reckon time. These included wet and dry seasons, social events (such as ball games), village ceremonial feastings, life passages (such as the initiation of boys to men and girls to women), as well as the deaths of important individuals in their communities. Such events were probably transmitted orally through successive generations and became part of the collective memory and histories of those societies. In cases where documentary records are lacking, oral history, ethnohistory, and archaeology are the primary data sources used in reconstructing the histories of many nonliterate societies.

Archaeology will invariably be the major source of information whenever native societies (that existed centuries before the arrival of the early Europeans) are the subject of investigations. This brings into sharp perspective the importance of archaeological time, which provides historical chronology for past societies through radiocarbon dating, stratigraphy, and seriation.

Radiocarbon dating (also called carbon dating or carbon-14 dating) is the determination of the approximate age of organic materials by measuring the amount of carbon-14 they contain. Plants take up atmospheric carbon dioxide by photosynthesis and are eaten by animals, so every living thing is constantly exchanging carbon-14 with its environment. Once it dies, however, this exchange stops, and the amount of carbon-14 gradually decreases through radioactive decay. This decay can be used to get a measure of how long ago a piece of once-living material died.

Stratigraphy is the study and interpretation of layered deposits. It is usually assumed, and is commonly true, that one layer is laid down upon the previous layer in an orderly progression through time creating a stratigraphy. By peeling away the different layers through excavation, archaeologists can use stratigraphic information to establish the relative ages of different deposits.

Seriation is a relative dating technique used to place artifacts in chronological order based on similarities in style. All three dating methods have been applied, whether singly or in combination, in our investigations of various pre-

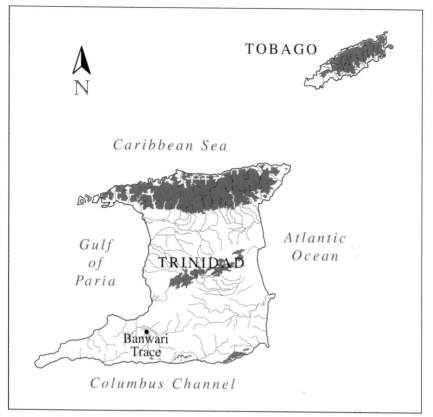

Figure 1.4. Banwari Trace, Trinidad. (Adapted from Boomert, *Trinidad and Tobago*. Used by permission.)

colonial sites in the Caribbean. However, the history of any past native society is more than marking time; it also involves understanding details of everyday life, reflected in the archaeological/historical record. An important example of this is Banwari Trace, where archaeological research has provided a wealth of information on both chronology as well as lifeways.

Banwari Trace

The oldest site in the West Indies is the seven-thousand-year-old Banwari Trace in southwest Trinidad (Figure 1.4). Therefore, the arrival of the Banwari Trace people in Trinidad (Boomert 2000), not the arrival of Christopher Columbus, marks the beginning of Caribbean history. Through archaeology, we know that the Banwari Trace inhabitants were actively engaged in hunting, gathering, and shell (mollusk) collecting. A considerable portion of the

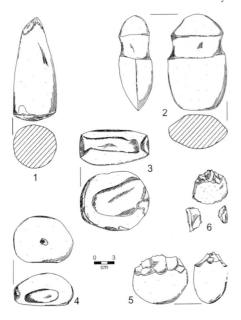

Figure 1.5. Stone artifacts from Banwari Trace: *1*, conical pestle; *2*, grooved ax; *3* and *4*, side ("faceted") grinders; *5*, chopper; *6*, utilized flakes. (Reproduced from Boomert, *Trinidad and Tobago*. Used by permission.)

shellfish collected was deposited in the immediate surroundings of the site. Objects associated with hunting and fishing found at the site include bone projectile points, most likely used for tipping arrows and fish spears, beveled peccary teeth used as fishhooks, and bipointed pencil hooks of bone that were intended to be attached in the middle to a fishing line (Boomert 2000). The ground stone tools may have been used for the processing of foods, especially vegetables. Tool types include blunt or pointed conical pestles, large grinding stones, and round to oval manos. The plant foods processed at the Banwari Trace site are unknown but probably included edible roots, palm starch, and seeds. The midden (refuse heap) has also yielded a large variety of small, irregular chips and cores made from quartz, flint, chert, and other rock materials. They include flake scrapers, cutters, small knives, blades, and piercers, which were probably used for a multitude of purposes, for example, the cutting of meat, scaling of fish, prying open of shells, scraping of skins, finishing of arrow shafts, and the processing of vegetable fibers for the making of basketry (Boomert 2000). Figure 1.5 shows a small sample of stone artifacts from Banwari Trace.

A significant discovery at Banwari Trace in 1969 was a human skeleton, dubbed Banwari Man. Lying on its left side, in a typical Amerindian crouched burial position along a northwest axis, Banwari Man was found 20 cm (7.8 in) below the surface (Harris 1971). Only two items were associated with the burial, a round pebble by the skull and needlepoint by the hip. The individual was apparently buried in a shell midden and subsequently covered by shell refuse. Based on its stratigraphic location in the site's archaeological deposits, the burial can be dated to the period shortly before the site was abandoned, approximately 3,400 B.C. Plans are afoot to conduct more detailed research on these remains, currently within the custody of the Life Sciences Department at the University of the West Indies, St. Augustine. Recent preliminary investigations of the Banwari remains indicated that the famous Banwari man could in fact be a woman (Coppa 2006, personal communication). Upon examining its third upper molar teeth, the physical anthropologist noticed that all the roots were formed and that there was a slight wear on the occlusal portion (Coppa 2006, personal communication). Subject to further verification, this suggests that Banwari man was a twenty-five- to thirty-year-old adult.

Without the presence of artifacts and other remains, archaeologists would find it difficult to reconstruct patterns of behavior of past societies in very early sites such as Banwari Trace. Archaeology has brought to life the long history of Trinidad prior to the arrival of Europeans. Ethnography (the study of cultures of living or contemporary peoples) can also be used in combination with archaeology to better understand past human behaviors. This may involve observing and documenting communities that are culturally and ethnically related to early Amerindian societies in the Caribbean, such as Arawak descendants who live in St. Cuthbert (Guyana) and Bernardsdorp (Suriname). Such studies can provide insights into cultural continuities or discontinuities relating to pottery manufacture, housing construction and agricultural practices. While these ethnographic studies do not always provide a one-to-one correlation between the past and the present (given the dramatic changes in technology and social organization in the New World since European colonization), they still can provide interesting insights into the histories of many past native societies.

Conclusion

The precolonial peoples of the Caribbean were dynamic, self-reflexive, and active human agents who modified and transformed their societies in definite relationships to one another (Miller and Tilley 1984) and were capable of devising "complex strategies to solve their problems and meet their goals," a perspective described by Elizabeth Brumfiel (1992:551–67) as "agent-centered." Clearly, the early indigenes of the Caribbean were not passive, timeless recipients of external European colonization but created their own histories, reflected in their dynamic social, economic, and political lifeways. We need to credit them with the same active intelligence and decision-making ability with which we credit ourselves. Archaeology, whether used solely or in combination with other techniques, is an indispensable toolkit for rewriting Caribbean history. The study of Banwari Trace, the site that represents the beginning of history in the Caribbean, is a fine example of this.

Myth 2

The Arawaks and Caribs Were the Two Major Groups in the Precolonial Caribbean

Some history books refer to the Arawaks and Caribs as the two major groups to have colonized the Caribbean. However, archaeological research has pointed to the presence of multiple cultural groups in the region before 1492, namely the Casimiroid, Ortoioroid, Saladoid, Barrancoid, Troumassan Troumassoid, Suazan Troumassoid, and Ostionoid peoples. Caribbean archaeologists have designated these various groups based on the names of sites where artifacts associated with the groups were first identified.

≈

Identifying and Naming Precolonial Peoples in the Caribbean

Traditional views of the precontact Caribbean, based in part on mistaken ethnohistoric perspectives, divided the archipelago between only two large and relatively homogenous groups: the Arawaks and the Caribs (Wilson 2007). While some history books (Rogonzinki 2000; Dookhan 2006) continue to refer to the Arawaks and Caribs as the two major Amerindian groups, Caribbean archaeologists have been able to identify multiple cultural groups based on artifact types. Attaching an identity to particular artifacts or monuments, most frequently expressed in terms of the ethnic groups, or peoples, who produced them has figured at the heart of archaeological enquiry (Hides 1996). While the identification of "cultures" from archaeological remains and their association with past ethnic groups is seen by many as hopelessly inadequate (Jones 1997), there is currently no better alternative, given that we are dealing with nonliterate groups, communities, and societies that existed thousands of years ago and therefore did not leave behind any tangible information concerning their names or ethnic identities. Even the task of ascribing names to contact-period groups, such as the Taínos and the Island-Caribs, has been fraught with significant challenges (see Hulme 1993). (See Chapters 3, 4, and 7.).

For example, in an attempt to differentiate the Caribs of the southern Caribbean from their counterparts in South America, Caribbean archaeologists have been referring to the former group as Island-Caribs (Keegan 1992; Rouse 1992). Even if Kalinago or Kalina is arguably the preferred cultural/ethnic identifier for this group, it should be borne in mind that these terms invariably refer to the living Caribs of Dominica (Ricardo Hernandez 2008, personal communication), with their usage stemming from the 17th-century linguistic studies of the Dominica Caribs by Father Raymond Guillaume Breton (Saunders 2005). Kalinago or Kalina cannot be usefully applied to the Carib Indians of Trinidad and Tobago let alone those of South America. The name Carib is a product of European cultural biases (see Chapter 7), but Caribbean archaeologists will continue to use it, given the lack of a better alternative.

The problem of names is not restricted to the Caribbean; it is in fact a worldwide phenomenon. For example, "American" usually refers to someone who is a citizen of the United States of America, even though the geographic term "the Americas" refers to North, South, and Central America. Many people identify themselves by national boundaries (e.g., Mexican, Nicaraguan, Venezuelan, Jamaican, or Trinidadian), despite the fact that these national identifiers mask the level of ethnic diversity in those countries. Others use more local terms (e.g., Floridian, Californian, Xinguano), their heritage (e.g., African American, Afro-Caribbean, Irish American), or their local group identity (e.g., Mehinaku, Makaritare, Carib) and so on.

Names and the Culture-Historical Approach

Caribbean archaeologists have sought to circumvent the problem of names by using artifactual assemblages relating primarily to pottery and stone artifact types to identify the presence or absence of major cultural groups. This is called the culture-historical approach and can be defined as an attempt by archaeologists to use approaches utilized by traditional historians, or simply projecting history back into periods when there was no writing (Drewett 1999). In other words, the culture-historical approach attempts to reconstruct the history of people based on detailed local sequences of artifacts and information about their geographic distribution (Drewett 1999). But there is also another step in the process. The cultures and peoples associated with certain artifactual types have also been given the name of the site where each artifact type was first described. For example, Saladoid was named after the site of Saladero in Venezuela, where its pottery characteristics were first identified and classified (Figure 2.1). For several decades, Caribbean archaeologists have been

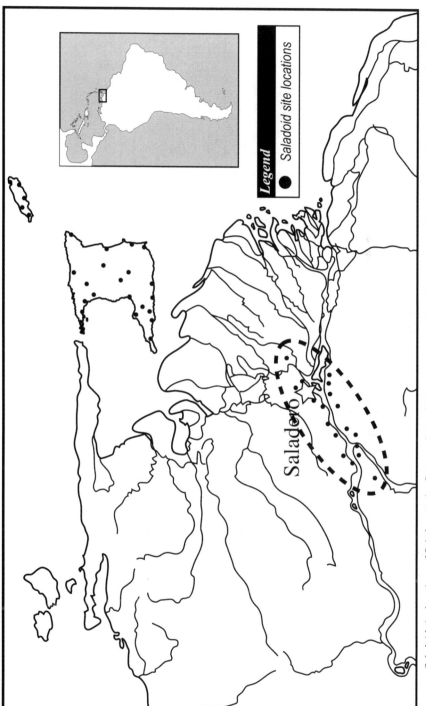

Figure 2.1. Saladoid site locations of Saladero in the Orinoco delta of Venezuela, northeastern South America. (Adapted from Boomert, *Trinidad and Tobago*. Used by permission.)

grouping pottery and lithic styles that shared a sufficient number of similarities into subseries (denoted by the *-an* suffix), and subseries were grouped into series (denoted by the *-oid* suffix) (Reid 2006). This classification was used to identify "peoples" and "cultures," which, according to Irving Rouse, the originator of this approach, represents "two sides of the coin, one consisting of a local population group and the other the cultural traits that define the group." For example, Saladoid is a series and Cedrosan is a subseries of the Saladoid series. Despite minor adjustments through the years, this system of classification remains an intrinsic part of scholarly research in the Caribbean to this day (Reid 2006) and will be used as the basis for the identification of the following precolonial groups in the Caribbean. Even as we adopt the series and subseries approach, we should be mindful that within this broad classification, there were several local groups that emerged throughout the Caribbean, identified by their distinctive artifact styles (Keegan 2007).

The rich and inviting nature of Caribbean ecosystems, the presence of several species of large, slow prey, the lack of terrestrial predators, an abundance of fisheries, estuaries, and mangrove swamps (Wilson 2007) and lack of competition for land and resources by other cultural groups may have been major pull factors for early migration into the Caribbean region. At the end of the Pleistocene, around twelve thousand years ago, and at the beginning of the Holocene, sea levels began to rise (Digerfeldt and Hendry 1987). It is possible that rising sea levels on the mainland reduced land areas, thereby forcing the human population into smaller spaces and convincing some to venture out to unknown islands (Wilson 2007).

Ortoiroids (5000–200 B.C.) and Casimiroids (4000–400 B.C.)

The first two groups of migrants to the Caribbean were the Ortoiroids and the Casimiroids. The Ortoiroids probably migrated from the Guianas in South America (Boomert 2000) while the Casimiroids may have come from Belize in Central America (Figure 2.2) (Saunders 2005). Named after Ortoire in eastern Trinidad, the Ortoiroids, arriving in the Caribbean around 5000 B.C. settled the Lesser Antilles to as far as Puerto Rico until 200 B.C. Taking their name for the archaeological type-site of Casimira in southwestern Hispaniola, the Casimiroid peoples lived between 4000 B.C. and 400 B.C. on the two largest islands of the Greater Antilles, Cuba and Hispaniola (modern-day Haiti and the Dominican Republic).

Archaic Period

Based on their artifact types, these two groups characteristically belong to the Archaic period in which permanent settlements were becoming more common

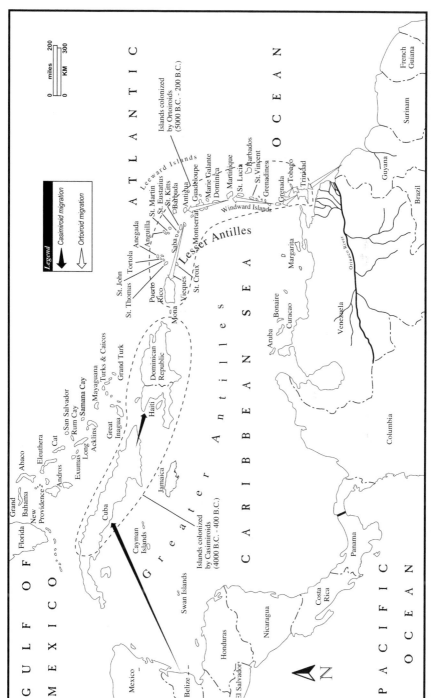

Figure 2.2. Ortoiroid and Casimiroid migration and colonization of the Caribbean.

and human groups were making the transition from hunting and gathering to agriculture. The Archaic period is usually defined by the presence of ground stone, shell, or both; a marine-oriented subsistence that followed a terrestrial hunting-based economy; and an emphasis on marine shell (mollusk) collecting (Davis 1982). Ortoiroid artifacts include spear points and barbs and also perforated animal teeth for stringing jewelry (Saunders 2005). Roughly made stone tools include manos, metates, pestles, and simple choppers, hammerstones, and coarsely chipped stone (Saunders 2005). Dated to about 5000 B.C., the Ortoiroid site of Banwari Trace site in south Trinidad is the oldest site in the Caribbean. Other Ortoiroid sites in Trinidad and Tobago include St. John's, Ortoire (both in Trinidad) and Milford (in Tobago). Two Ortoiroid sites, with a relative abundance of edge-grinding pebbles have been found in Martinique. Some twenty-four Ortoiroid shell middens have, to date, been found in Antigua, mainly in areas suitable for fishing and shellfish gathering.

Casimiroid stone tools, which are similar to those of the Ortoiroids, include sophisticated blades, used as spear points to hunt sloths and manatees; conical pestles and mortars to prepare food and a variety of possible ritual implements such as stone balls, disks, and daggerlike objects, as well as elaborate stone beads and shell jewelry (Figure 2.3) (Saunders 2005). Casimiroid sites, which date to around 2660 B.C., have been identified on the north and south coasts of Haiti (Keegan 1994). In the Dominican Republic, Casimiroid sites are located in river valleys and along the coast. It appears that Casimiroid ground-stone tools in south-central Cuba were first shaped by flaking, which was then followed by pecking and grinding (Keegan 1994).

The Ortoiroids and Casimiroids were Potters

Traditionally, both the Ortoiroids and Casimiroids as Archaic peoples were defined by the absence of pottery. However, recent studies have challenged this assumption by demonstrating that both groups were making pottery at least two thousand years before the arrival of the Saladoids. There is also evidence to suggest that they were engaged in plant cultivation, as wild grain and fruit trees were established foods during the Archaic period in the Caribbean (Newson 1993). The manos, metates, and pestles of the Casimiroid and Ortoiroid were likely used in preparing foods that were probably the products of agriculture. In the New World tropics, there is a strong correlation between the making of clay pots and agriculture (Rice 2006). The pottery found on Archaic sites throughout the Caribbean offers further tantalizing evidence of farming activities. Over time, the Casimiroid descendants evolved into the Ostionoids, who later became the Taínos while the Ortoiroids may have been assimilated by the Saladoids who migrated to the Caribbean from South America around 500 B.C. However, the notion of Archaic assimilation for the entire Caribbean has been disputed (Chanlatte Baik 1986). The evidence suggests that there

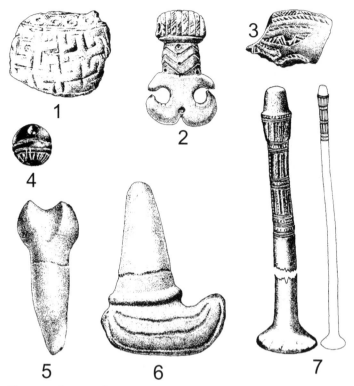

Figure 2.3. Casimiroid art: *1* and *3*, fragments of stone bowls; *2*, shell pendant; *4*, stone bead; *5*, peg-shaped stone; *6*, hook-shaped stone; *7*, wooden batons. (Reproduced from Rouse, *The Taínos*. Used by permission.)

was a long period of transculturation rather than assimilation between the Saladoid-La Hueca peoples and the Ortoiroids on the eastern half of Puerto Rico, which eventually gave rise to the Elenan Ostionoid series (Chanlatte Baik 1986).

Saladoids (500 B.C.–A.D. 600)

Origins of the Saladoids

The origins of the Saladoid people have been traced to the banks of the Orinoco River in northeastern Venezuela (Rouse 1989). As early as 2100 B.C., villages of agriculturalists, who used pottery vessels to cook their food, had been established along the middle Orinoco. During the ensuing two thousand years, their population increased and they expanded downriver and outward along the Orinoco tributaries (Keegan 1992). Upon entering the Caribbean around 500 B.C. the Saladoids quickly settled all the islands of the Caribbean from Trinidad and Tobago in the south to as far north as Puerto Rico (Figures 2.4

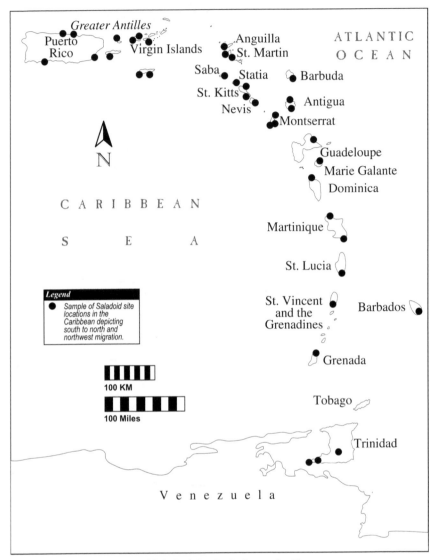

Figure 2.4. Early and late period Saladoid sites in the Lesser Antilles.

and 2.5). The distinctive pottery styles of the Saladoids are red, white-on-red (WOR), black and polychrome paint, and zone-incised-crosshatchings (ZIC) (Figure 2.6). These pottery styles have been the primary benchmark used to trace the migratory route of the Saladoids from northeast South America to the eastern extremity of the Greater Antilles.

Saladoids practiced a mixed economy of root-crop agriculture, hunting of land animals, fishing, and mollusk (shellfish) collecting. The presence of clay

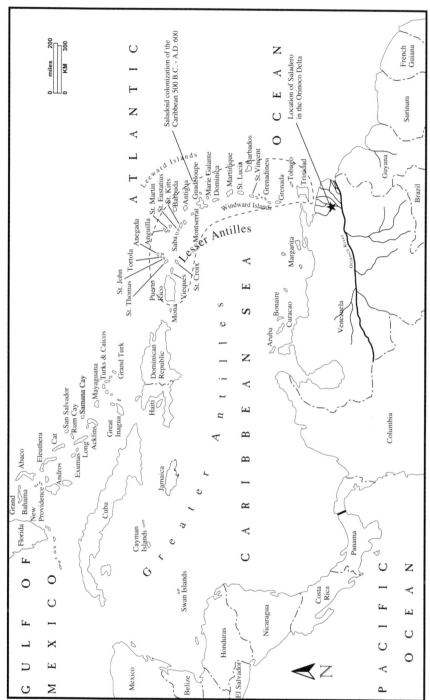

Figure 2.5. Saladoid-La Hueca colonization of the Caribbean. (Adapted from Haviser, "Settlement Strategies." Used by permission of Haviser.)

Figure 2.6. Asymmetrical Saladoid vessel from Erin, Trinidad, decorated with white-on-red motifs. (Reproduced from Boomert, *Trinidad and Tobago.* Used by permission.)

griddles suggests that bitter manioc was cultivated for cassava bread at this time, as it was by later groups, such as the Ostionoids and the Taínos. However, they did not introduce cultivable plants to the Caribbean. Botanical studies investigating preserved starch grains on grinding tools have demonstrated that virtually all of the plants that were supposedly introduced by the Saladoids were already being cultivated by their Archaic predecessors (Pagan Jiménez 2007, personal communication).

Social Complexity

The Saladoid peoples are assumed to have had an egalitarian, or tribally based, society (Curet 1996; Siegel 1992). Villages are generally not known to reflect

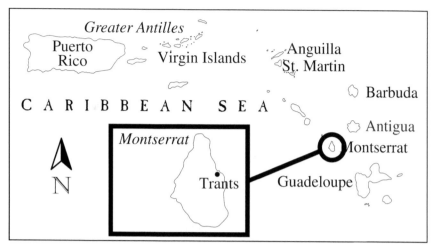

Figure 2.7. Trants, Montserrat, in the northern Leeward Islands. (Adapted from Watters, "Archaeology of Trants, Montserrat." Courtesy of the Carnegie Museum of Natural History.)

the level of size-rank hierarchy characteristic of the Taínos in Puerto Rico and Hispaniola, which is further evidence of egalitarianism. Moreover, burials from this time period lack the elaborate grave offerings that would indicate difference in status among those interred. However, archaeological investigations of the very large site of Trants in Montserrat (Figure 2.7) suggest that the Saladoids may have been more socially complex than is commonly assumed (Petersen 1996). The village itself (circular or ring pattern) is about 60,000 m² (64,560 ft²) with an overall artifact distribution (including outlying areas) of 600,000 m² (645,600 ft²) making Trants one of the largest Saladoid sites in the Caribbean (Watters 2007, personal communication). The site may have been occupied by as many as two hundred to three hundred people for eight hundred years (Petersen 1996). It is possible that Trants, given its large size, was a regional center for Saladoid communities on nearby islands in the Lesser Antilles. But this argument is tentative at best, given the presence of other large Saladoid sites in nearby Antigua such as Indian Creek and Royall's (Watters 2007, personal communication).

The Saladoids were not monolithic. Multiple local groups, identifiable by different pottery styles, either entered or developed in the Antilles. The best evidence for such local-group differences is the absence of painted pottery at the Sorcé site on Vieques Island of eastern Puerto Rico (Chanlatte Baik and Narganes Storde 1990) and the presence of zone punctuate pottery at Hope Estate, St. Martin (Haviser 1997). These two sites, coupled with the site at Punta Candalero in eastern Puerto Rico, show that at least some groups did not produce the full range of the Cedrosan Saladoid pottery decorations (Keegan 2000) typically characterized by WOR painting. However, some archaeologists (Chanlatte Baik 1981, 1986; Chanlatte Baik and Narganes Storde 1983, 1985; Oliver 1999) have seriously questioned whether all pottery styles contemporaneous with the Saladoids in the Caribbean are in fact Saladoid. For instance, the pottery discovered at Vieques (immediately east of Puerto Rico), identified as La Hueca complex, differs markedly from typical WOR Saladoid ceramics in designs, motifs, representations, and vessel forms. In addition, a large number of high-quality lapidary pieces made of foreign materials (probably from as far away as Brazil or the Guianas) were discovered in the La Hueca complex, which have not previously been reported for the Caribbean (Curet 2005). As a result La Hueca has been interpreted as representing a separate migration from South America that occurred simultaneously with Saladoid migration also from the mainland (Curet 2005).

Lapidary Trade

Saladoid technology was simple and apparently available to everyone. There is evidence for wood, stone, bone and shell working, as well as lapidary (trading of exotic or precious stones), weaving, and pottery making. Long-distance trading expeditions by canoe required effective planning and coordination (Keegan 2000). Concerning lapidary trade, excavations in Blanchisseuse, north Trinidad in March 2007 unearthed a stone (Figure 2.8) derived from a fine-grained, acidic, extrusive igneous, volcanic rock probably from the Lesser Antilles (Wilson 2007). While the function of this stone is unclear, the fact that it was imported into Trinidad from islands north of Trinidad in the Lesser Antilles suggests that it was of considerable cultural significance to the Saladoid inhabitants of Blanchisseuse. However, objects do not necessarily have to be imported to be considered significant in our interpretation of Saladoid culture. A case in point is a Saladoid pendant found at Blanchisseuse in March 2005 by an archaeology crew of the University of the West Indies, St. Augustine (Figure 2.9). The oval-shaped pendant is 40.9 mm (1.6 in) long, 3.2 to 3.6 mm (0.13 to 0.14 in) thick, and 11.5 to 27.8 mm (0.5 to 1.0 in) wide. Its well-defined hole, through which a string might have been strung in order for the adornment to hang around the wearer's neck, has a diameter of 4 mm (0.15 in). Made from schist, a medium grade metamorphic rock, which is commonly found in the Northern Range of Trinidad in close proximity to the site, the pendant was probably not imported. Nevertheless, it has provided useful insights into the personal adornment habits of the early Saladoid settlers of Blanchisseuse.

Going farther afield to the northern Lesser Antilles, information from excavated beads in Trants, Montserrat strongly suggests that Trants was a precolonial lithic bead manufacturing center specializing in carnelian beads. It may be that certain islands in the Lesser Antilles, such as Montserrat (carnelian)

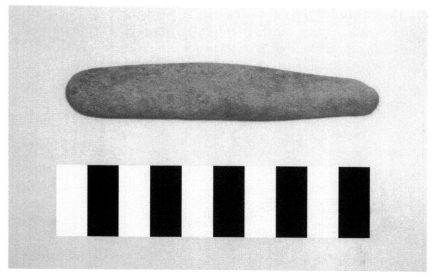

Figure 2.8. Lapidary stone found at Blanchisseuse, north Trinidad. (Scale 10 cm [4 in].)

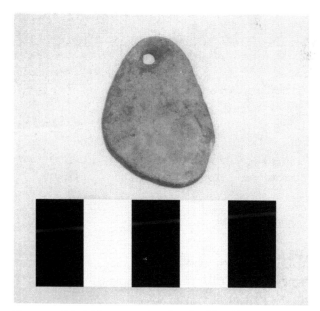

Figure 2.9. Saladoid stone pendant found at Blanchisseuse, north Trinidad. (Scale 5 cm [2 in].)

and Grenada (amethyst) were specializing in the production of lithic beads primarily for offshore trade (Watters and Scaglion 1994). However, not all of the stones used in lapidary trade were imported from outside of specific island territories. A stellar example of intraisland lapidary trade is Antigua. Two archaeological sites, Elliot's and Royall's, were excavated between 1997 and 1999 (Figure 2.10), both of which appear to have flourishing lapidary industries. While the abundance of beads, pendants, and zemis made from shells, carnelian and diorite (all of local origin) clearly suggests that there was intraisland lapidary trade on the island of Antigua, the presence of amethyst, nephrite, serpentine, and turquoise (which are not local) imply that trade or exchange existed between Antigua and other parts of the circum-Caribbean and possibly the Americas during Saladoid time (Murphy et al. 2000). In fact, there is increasing evidence for the movement of precolonial peoples, goods, and ideas between the insular Caribbean and the Isthmo-Colombian area (Colombia, Panama, and Costa Rica). Jadeite axes from Antigua recently were sourced to the Motagua Valley in Nicaragua; gold objects have been traced to Colombia; and many of the personal adornments made from shell, stone, and bone have shapes and decorations that are identical to those found at the same time in this region (Keegan 2007).

Religion and Cosmology

South American cosmology, clearly reflected in Saladoid religion, was profoundly polytheistic and animistic. It revolves around a common belief in a vast number of spirits related to nature, the forest, the sky, rivers and mountains. Symbols and mythological themes also depict a flexible distinction between humans and animals, with human-animal transformations being the norm rather than the exception (Reid 2004). The Saladoids transformed their lifeways developed along the river banks of South America to suit an island environment. Perhaps this transformation was most evident in their understanding of themselves, their gods, and their cosmos. The most important symbolic creatures of the mainland—the jaguar and caiman—were replaced with a system of symbols that came from other creatures such as dogs, bats, and humans (Wilson 1997).

Saladoid potters showed a special fondness for the representation of personages, animals, and fantastic creatures. The bodies and heads of zoomorphic, anthropomorphic, and anthropozoomorphic figures and fantastical creatures were used to decorate many of their ceramic vessels that were often used in ceremonial feastings in the central plazas of villages. All of these clearly suggest a complex system of supernatural and mythological representations (Figure 2.11) (Rodriguez 1997; Reid 2004).

Figure 2.10. Elliot's and Royall's in Antigua. (Adapted from Murphy et al., "Pre-Columbian Gems," 236. Used by permission of Murphy.)

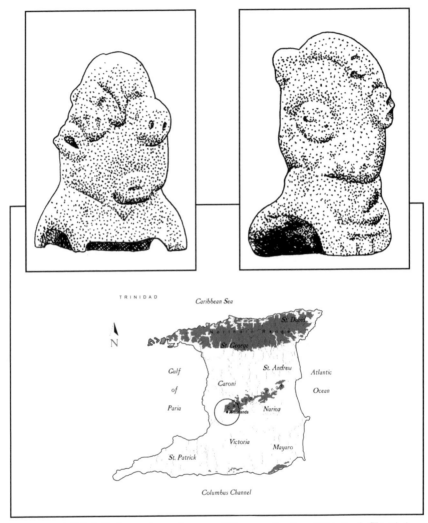

Figure 2.11. A Saladoid adorno, shown from two different angles, from Whitelands, Trinidad. The figure probably represents a bat.

Village Layout

Saladoid villages were highly structured places, usually discerned archaeologically by the presence of middens arranged around a large space, carefully cleared of refuse (Siegel 1996). This cleared space was the central plaza and was the venue for ritual displays and ceremonial feasts. Human burials were sometimes interred in the central plaza. Examples of this village layout throughout the Antilles include Punta Candalero and Maisabel in Puerto Rico, Sorcé on Vieques Island and Golden Rock site in St. Eustatius.

Saladoid Village Layout in Trinidad and Tobago

Trinidad and Tobago, one of the first migratory stops for many Saladoid communities en route to the rest of the Caribbean, has approximately forty Saladoid sites, many of which are middens (Boomert 2000) (Figure 2.12). Located in north Trinidad, the 2-ha (5-a) site of Marianne Estate in Blanchisseuse is generally considered as one of the largest Saladoid sites on the island. The site has also been subjected to sporadic archaeological research from 1959—a year after it was first discovered by H. C. Potter during the widening of the Paria main road—to 2008, when the southern side was surveyed and excavated by the history/archaeology students from the University of the West Indies, St. Augustine. Shovel test pits in 1999 suggested the presence of a village community centered around a central plaza at Blanchisseuse (Figure 2.13), which is typical of Saladoid village layouts throughout the Caribbean. In Figure 2.13, areas with sparser quantities of pottery may be the location of the central plaza while areas with heavier quantities of pottery may have been the residential areas of precolonial Blanchisseuse. Multiple radiocarbon dates indicate that the Blanchisseuse site was continuously inhabited by the Saladoid people from eighteen hundred to fourteen hundred years ago (Reid 2003). Another thoroughly researched Saladoid site in Trinidad is Manzanilla on the east coast of the island. At Manzanilla, archaeologists from Leiden University found a village layout, typical of the other Saladoid villages throughout the Caribbean (Figure 2.14). In Figure 2.14, larger dark circles represent habitation areas of the Manzanilla Saladoids, while the white dots in the middle of the diagram depict the "swept area," or central plaza.

General Comments

Saladoid pottery, in terms of vessel shapes and decorative techniques, shows strong affinities with pottery that was being manufactured along the Orinoco River at this time. In this regard, the Saladoids probably shared a common ancestry with the Arawaks of South America. However, research indicates that the relationship between these peoples was far more complex than previously thought. There is also solid evidence of the development of multiple local groups within the broad Saladoid cultural classification and extensive lapidary trading within the Caribbean and the Isthmo-Colombian region. This supports the belief that the Saladoids were not simply Arawaks from South America but a multicultural society that developed in the Caribbean islands from 500 B.C. to A.D. 600.

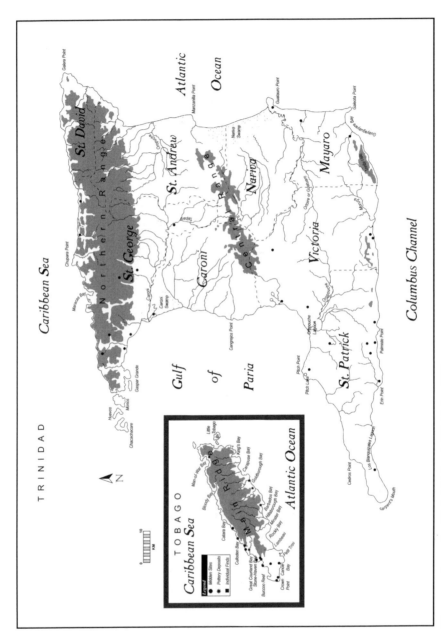

Figure 2.12. A sample of Saladoid sites in Trinidad and Tobago.

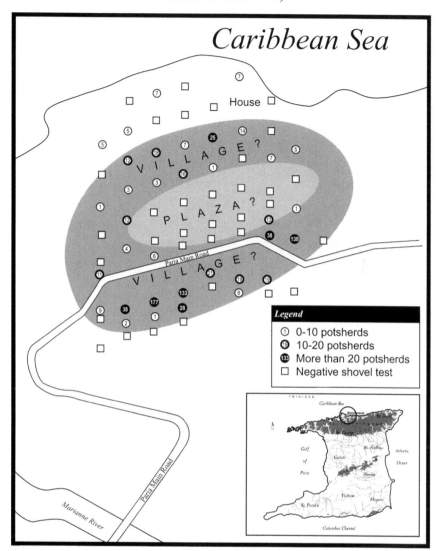

Figure 2.13. Saladoid village layout at Blanchisseuse, north Trinidad (based on pottery densities). (Adapted from Stokes and Steadman. Used by permission.)

Barrancoids (A.D. 350–650)

The Barrancoid peoples take their name from the site of Barrancas on the banks of the lower Orinoco River in Venezuela (Saunders 2005). Barrancoid culture seemed to have developed out of the local Saladoid tradition in Venezuela between 1500 B.C. and 1000 B.C. Its peoples moved northward to the

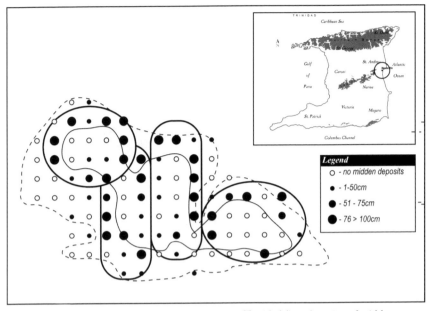

Figure 2.14. Saladoid village layout at Manzanilla, east Trinidad (based on size of midden deposits). (Used by permission of Marc Dorst.)

mouth of the Orinoco river delta, perhaps displacing or bypassing other Saladoid communities as they went (Saunders 2005). Like the Saladoids, they cultivated cassava, produced pottery and lived in villages. Throughout the Caribbean, their influence was quite extensive, as they reached as far north as Vieques (Allaire 1997) and Puerto Rico (Figure 2.15). Like the Saladoids, the Barrancoid peoples were expert canoeists and appear to have been masters of long distance trade. Sites such as Sorcé on Vieques and others in Montserrat and Tobago have been referred to by archaeologists as Saladoid/Barrancoid ports of trade (Saunders 2005).

The Barrancoid peoples were among the most dynamic population in eastern Venezuela and adjacent areas and would eventually settle Trinidad around A.D. 350 (Allaire 1997). The mechanisms by which Barrancoid influences are associated with Saladoid pottery remain poorly understood, and the relationship between the two styles is problematic. A common tendency is to describe ceramics of this period as Saladoid with Barrancoid influences (Allaire 1997). Nevertheless, the discovery of Barrancoid pottery in Cedrosan Saladoid sites in Trinidad and Tobago, and of typically Saladoid ZIC (zone-incised cross-hatching) pottery in the Lower Orinoco locations suggests trade as an important mechanism. No independent Barrancoid settlements have been found either on Trinidad or Paria (Boomert 2003), which further suggests that after

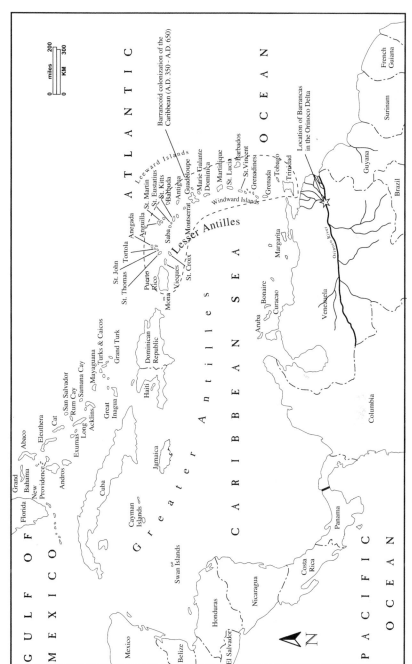

Figure 2.15. Barrancoid colonization of the Caribbean.

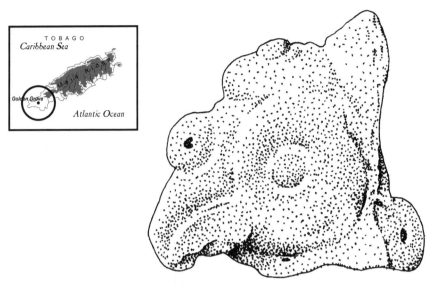

Figure 2.16. Barrancoid-influenced Saladoid adorno from Golden Grove, Tobago.

A.D. 350 a significant element of the Barrancoid population went to live in Saladoid villages, where they intermarried and interacted with the Saladoids (Boomert 2003).

The Barrancoid-influenced Saladoid pottery, referred to as the modified Saladoid tradition (Boomert 2003), differed little from the Saladoid pottery in terms of manufacture and choice of temper. However, striking differences are evident in vessel shapes and ornamentation. Barrancoid pottery has often been characterized as the baroque phase of Saladoid stylistic evolution, typically represented in its modeled incised decoration found on handles, adornos with anthropomorphic and zoomorphic hands, feet, and faces (Figure 2.16), as well as incense burners, probably used for the ritual taking of hallucinogens. Around A.D. 650, the Barrancoid culture faded in the Caribbean. The reasons for this are unclear, and it is hoped that more detailed research will eventually provide definitive answers.

Troumassan Troumassoids (A.D. 500–1000)

A distinction is made here between the early Troumassoid peoples, called Troumassan Troumassoids, and the later Troumassoids, referred to as Suazan Troumassoids. The Troumassan Troumassoid peoples, who had culturally evolved from the Saladoids in the Lesser Antilles, are named after the type-site of Troumassée in St. Lucia. Troumassan Troumassoid subseries appear to have developed differently in the northerly Leeward and Virgin Islands than in the more southerly Windward Islands (Figure 2.17) (Boomert 2003).

The Troumassan Troumassoid subseries in the Leeward Islands and Guadeloupe evolved into local Mamorean subseries from A.D. 800–1200 and these are well represented in Antigua and the other Leeward Islands. Named after the Mamora Bay pottery type on Antigua, the Mamorean subseries reflected some Cedrosan Saladoid elements, although this became progressively less overtime. Red-slipped surfaces gradually replaced the bicolor and polychrome painting. The bicolored painting in the Mamora Bay style was now simplified. Incisions were broad-lined with external curvilinear designs. Cedrosan Saladoid style handles had completely disappeared and lugs were rare (Hofman et al. 2007). The geographic reach of the Troumassan Troumassoids was not extended to the Virgin Islands, which had pottery belonging to the Magens Bay subseries. The Magens Bay subseries is named after Magens Bay in St. Thomas (U.S. Virgin Islands). Given that the Magens Bay ceramics display striking similarities with those of eastern Puerto Rico, where Ostionoid societies were beginning to emerge (Saunders 2005; Allaire 1997), this subseries is generally classified as part of the Elenan Ostionoid series. There is evidence of trade and cultural exchanges between the developing Ostionoid societies in the Greater Antilles and the late precolonial settlers of the Virgin Islands (Hofman et al. 2007). By A.D. 1200, both the Magens Bay subseries in the Virgin Islands and the Mamorean subseries in the Leewards had been so influenced by the Ostionoid cultures in Puerto Rico to the east that they came to be classified by some archaeologists (Rouse 1992) as Eastern Taínos (see Figure 3.3). Despite this, Taíno classifications for the Caribbean usually terminate at the eastern end of Puerto Rico (see Figure 3.1), as there is still no general consensus as to whether the material culture of islands east of Puerto Rico was Taíno or simply Taíno-influenced.

The Troumassan Troumassoids in the Windward Islands differed considerably from their neighbors to the north in their more diverse settlement patterns and pottery types. In the Windward Islands, what is called the Troumassan Troumassoid pottery, like its Saladoid predecessors, was painted red, black, and white, often outlined with curvilinear incised lines (Figure 2.18). They also had unpainted curvilinear incision and like the Saladoids they had wedge-shaped lugs. The pottery is cruder and plainer than discovered during previous time periods, and the zoomorphic adornos and loop handles for the most part disappeared. Vessels are fitted with legs, pedestals, or annular (ring-shaped) bases (Keegan 2000). The Barrancoid influence of stylistic modeling seems to have disappeared but other elements remained (Saunders 2005). The marked decrease in pottery quality and the simplification of decoration begin-

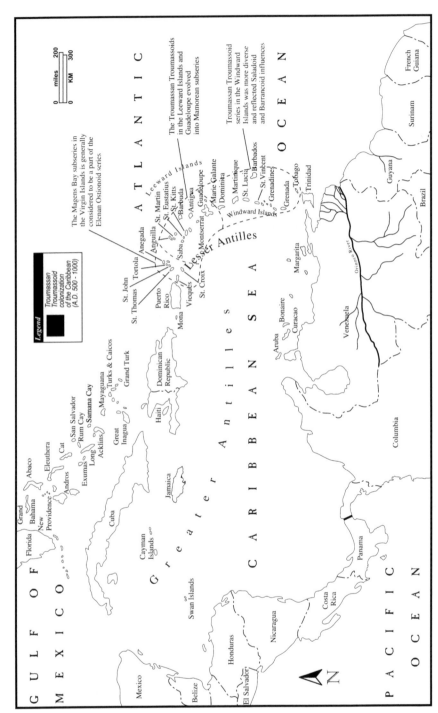

Figure 2.17. Troumassoid colonization of the Caribbean.

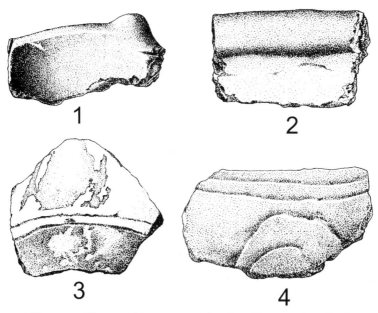

Figure 2.18. Troumassan Troumassoid pottery: *1*, wedge-shaped lug on a triangular rim; *2*, red-painted ridge inside a rim; *3*, white design on badly worn red slip; *4*, curvilineal incised design. (Reproduced from Rouse, *The Taínos*. Used by permission.)

ning with the eighth-century Troumassan Troumassoid subseries display many stylistic similarities shared by the later Barrancoid styles of coastal Venezuela (Allaire 1997). Clay spindle whorls first appeared at this time, which suggests an increased growing of cotton and trade in the finished items. There were specific adaptations by local societies to their islands that allowed them to expand territorially. This meant that they depended more on farming and fishing and less on gathering (Saunders 2005). In Martinique, an increased production of salt and cotton (Allaire 1990) may explain why Troumassan Troumassoid inhabitants on the island spread out from the humid and fertile (Boomert 2003) northeastern part of Martinique to occupy the more arid southeastern section (Saunders 2005). To date, the most completely excavated Troumassan Troumassoid site is the Paquemar on Martinique (Allaire 1997). The finds from this period in southern Martinique and northern St. Lucia are so similar as to suggest that the two areas functioned as an interaction sphere (Rouse 1992).

Suazan Troumassoids (A.D. 1000–1450)

Taking their name from the Savanne Suazey site on Grenada, the Suazan Troumassoids or Suazeys made their appearance in the southernmost Windward Islands, from Martinique to Tobago (Figure 2.19) around A.D. 1000, disappearing from the landscape about 1450. Due to similarities between Suazey pottery and the pottery of earlier Troumassoids, the pottery styles of the former are generally classified as a subseries of the Troumassoid series; hence the term Suazan Troumassoid. A.D. 1450 is generally considered as the termination of Suazan Troumassoid culture, as in southeastern Martinique the radiocarbon dates abruptly ended at this time. No European trade objects have been found at Suazan Troumassoid sites, either in Martinique or on the other French islands, which is further evidence that the Suazan Troumassoids experienced their demise before the arrival of the Spaniards in the late fifteenth century (Rouse 1992).

Evolving from its predecessor, the Troumassan Troumassoid, Suazan Troumassoid pottery is characterized by simple and bulky plain vessels, scratched surfaces, finger-indented rims, and finger-red painted and incised wares (Figure 2.20). They are also occasional flat human-head adornos with flaring pierced ears (Allaire 1997). Suazan Troumassoid ceramics may represent a general decline in technological production and artistic style from the earlier Troumassan Troumassoid tradition, though continuities exist. The attachment of legs to vessels and footed cassava griddles first introduced during the earlier Troumassoid Period continued to be made. Other Suazan Troumassoid items include clay spindle whorls, figurines, stone pestles, shell celts, and gouges, as well as clay cylinders that may have been incense burners (Saunders 2005). However, the presence of Caliviny pottery, which seems to be Suazan Troumassoid fineware, challenges the notion of Suazey technological deterioration. Caliviny pottery is tempered with medium-size grit with a surface finish that is achieved by burnishing without properly scraping and finishing the surfaces before burnishing (Bullen 1965). Thick walled cazuela vessels with red-painted bodies and above the shoulders repeated geometric designs in black and red paint applied on a buff surface also characterize a number of Caliviny pots (Bullen 1965). In Amerindian societies, coarseware was used for domestic purposes while fineware was invariably associated with ceremonial feasting.

Settlements are situated along the coast where they are close to shell-rich mangroves and offshore coral reefs. Massive footed griddles attest to manioc cultivation and the making of cassava bread (Keegan 2000). Suazan Troumassoid culture is arguably an Amazonian adaptation to a tropical island environment (Allaire 1991). Their subsistence was based on the same slash-and-burn cultivation of bitter cassava, complemented by hunting and fishing (Allaire 1991). Permanent sites are found along the coast close to water sources. Demonstrably, the Suazan Troumassoids had a preference for level terrain and good agricultural land. A prime example of this is the Lover's Retreat site in

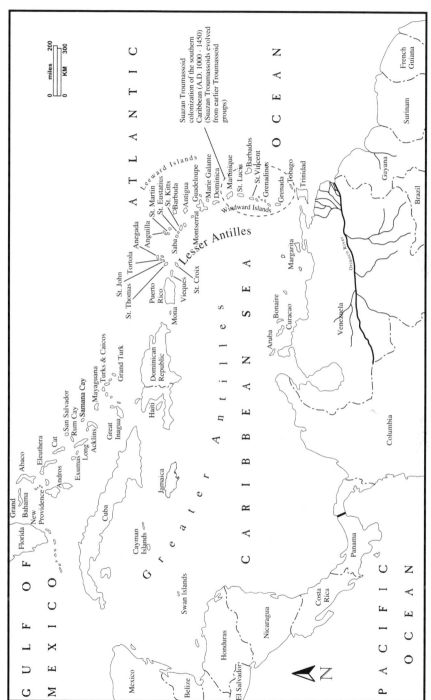

Figure 2.19. Suazan Troumassoid colonization of the southern Caribbean.

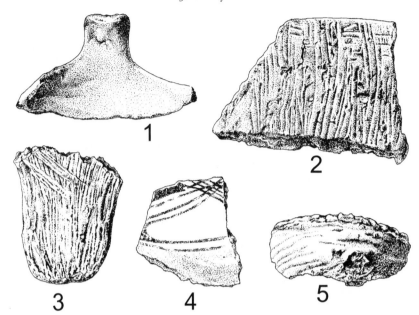

Figure 2.20. Suazan Troumassoid pottery: *1,* peg-shaped lug on the end of the bowl; *2,* scarified rim sherd; *3,* scarified griddle leg; *4,* vessel body that is red-slipped and surmounted by a linear black design on a plain surface (this type of potsherd is called Caliviny polychrome); *5,* simple hemispherical bowl with a finger-impressed rim. (Reproduced from Rouse, *The Taínos.* Used by permission.)

Tobago (Figure 2.21), which has been subjected to archaeological investigations from 1943 to 2005 (Reid 2005a).

There is still some uncertainty as to whether both the Mamorean and Magens Bay Troumassoid subseries in the northern Lesser Antilles also evolved into Suazan Troumassoid subseries like their counterparts in Windward Islands, or whether they transitioned directly from earlier Troumassoid cultures to Ostionoids. What seems certain, however, is that the Leeward Islands were evolving pottery styles more similar to those found in the Greater Antilles (Allaire 1997). A Taíno-influenced site, dated to A.D. 1300, has recently been discovered on Saba in the Leeward Islands. Most of this influence appears related to items of ritual importance, such as large three-pointer *zemis,* a *duho,* a possible hallucinogen-snuffing tube, and so-called human face masks (Saunders 2005).

It is still a mystery as to why the Suazey culture disappeared in A.D. 1450, even if we accept the fact that there was a general decline in native populations throughout the Caribbean in the century prior to European contact (Curet 1992). One school of thought argues that small island environments are prone

Figure 2.21. Lover's Retreat, Tobago.

to unpredictable population shifts, simply because their inhabitants are highly mobile (Allaire 1997). An analogous situation is the mysterious disappearance of the Laurentian Iroquois population form the lower St. Lawrence River between the time of Jacques Cartier's visit in the 1530s and Champlain's voyages seventy years later (Allaire 1997), although European diseases may have helped decimate that population. Whatever the reason for Suazey's sudden disappearance, the evidence suggests that there was an "ethnic revolution" in the Windward Islands in the fifteenth century as Island-Caribs moved into the vacuum left by the Suazan Troumassoid culture (Figure 2.22). While the Suazan Troumassoids may have disappeared as an identifiable cultural group after A.D. 1450, it is possible that some members of the group became what some Caribbean scholars describe as Arawak-speaking Igneris, among whom the Island-Caribs of the Windward islands settled.

Island-Caribs (A.D. 1450–the present)

Although Suazey was originally identified as the pottery made by the Island-Caribs, it now appears that Suazan Troumassoid pottery is not Island-Carib, as Suazan Troumassoid pottery is an entirely precolonial phenomenon that

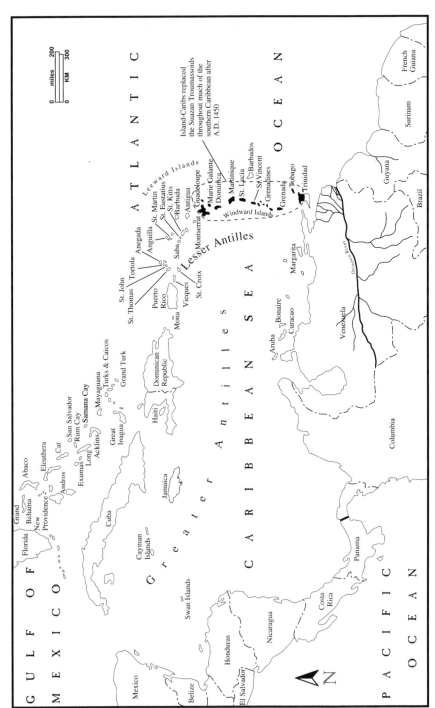

Figure 2.22. Island–Carib colonization of the southern Caribbean.

disappeared in A.D. 1450. Recent research has revealed that the Cayoid pottery style, named after Cayo in St. Vincent, may relate to the Island-Caribs. At the end of precolonial times, the Cayoid pottery, and other Guiana related styles, appeared in the Windward Islands of Tobago and St. Vincent (Boomert 1986). Characteristic features of the Cayoid pottery include incisions on a flat rim, cone-shaped necks, and bodies typical of appliqué decorations. Many of the Cayoid pots are tempered with *caraipe* or *kwep* in Amazonia and the coastal Guianas (Boomert 1986). This pottery, found in association with contact-period materials such as glass and metals, has been tentatively associated with the Island-Carib occupation of the Windward Islands. It also shows some strong similarities in decoration and shape to the Kariabo pottery style of the Guianas (Boomert 1986; Hofman et al. 2007), a group that may be culturally affiliated to the Island-Caribs.

Barbados is omitted from the Island-Carib colonization (Figure 2.22) as the island seems to have been depopulated before the arrival of Europeans (Drewett 1991). Unlike most of the larger Caribbean islands, when Europeans reached Barbados no encounters were recorded. The Amerindian population may have left before the Europeans arrived. Alternatively they may have moved to safer islands in advance of Spanish slavers who, following a *cédula real* issued by Charles V in 1515, were scouring the eastern Caribbean for Indian slaves to replace the thousands dying in the Cuban mines (Drewett 1991). The date of European landing on Barbados is uncertain. Barbados is omitted on Juan de la Cosa's map of 1500. In 1542 it appears on John Rotz's chart 17 as Beruados and on chart 18 as Isla de Beruados. Richard Ligon describes some Indians living in Barbados in 1647 but states that they were brought from other islands and the mainland (Drewett 1991). Despite this, several precolonial sites relating to the Saladoid, Barrancoid, Troumassan Troumassoid, and Suazan Troumassoid periods have been identified on the island of Barbados, underscoring the extent to which this largely coral island was intensively inhabited for several hundred years before the arrival of the first Europeans (Drewett 1991) (Figure 2.23). Shell technology figured prominently in the Amerindian toolkit of precolonial Barbados, primarily because of the shortage of hard stones on the island (Figures 2.24 and 2.25).

Ostionoids (A.D. 600–1200)

Named after the Ostiones site in Puerto Rico, the Ostionoids developed in the northern Caribbean from A.D. 600 to 1200 and by A.D. 1200 had evolved into the Taínos whom Columbus encountered in the northern Caribbean in 1492 (see Figures 4.4 and 4.7). The Ostionoid tradition itself was a uniquely Caribbean phenomenon, with none of the mainland characteristics of the Sala-

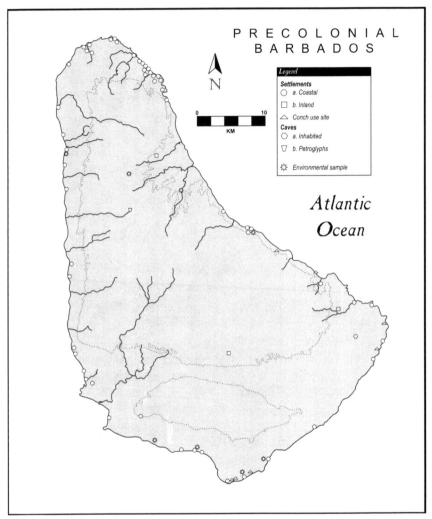

Figure 2.23. Distribution of precolonial settlement sites, conch use sites, utilized caves, and environmental sample locations in Barbados.

doids (Saunders 2005). They were farmers, potters, and villagers with socially complex societies. However, various other pottery styles within the inclusive Ostionoid tradition have been noted, leading to the creation of subseries or smaller groups called the Ostionan, Elenan, Meillacan, Chican, and Palmetto peoples (Figure 2.26).

Ostionan pottery (Figure 2.27) is characterized by simple black smudging, very basic modeling, and an orange red slip applied to the whole of the typically thin and hard ceramic vessel. It is widely referred to as redware (Saunders

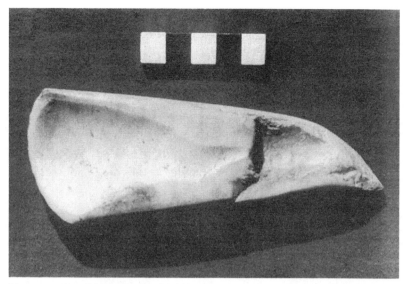

Figure 2.24. Conch (*Strombus gigas*) ax-adze from Silver Sands, Barbados (scale 5 cm [2 in]).

Figure 2.25. Conch (*Strombus gigas*) ax-adze from Silver Sands, Barbados (scale 5 cm [2 in]).

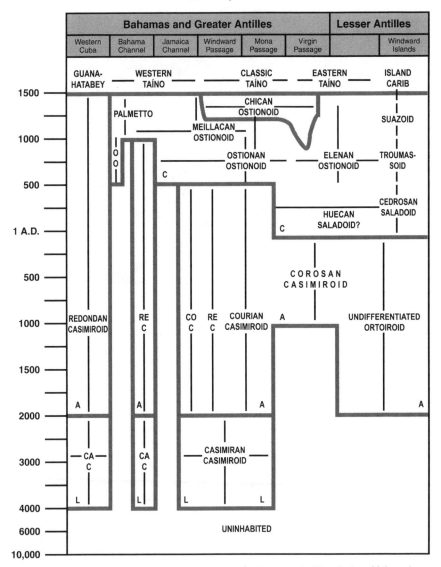

Figure 2.26. Chronology of the series and subseries of cultures in the West Indies. (Adapted from Rouse, *The Taínos*. Used by permission.)

2005). Ostionan people appear to have been the first human settlers to colonize Jamaica around A.D. 650, with the Ostionan site of Little River in the parish of St. Ann being the earliest known on the island. While the Ostionan Ostionoids occupied western Puerto Rico, Elenan Ostionoids settled all over the eastern half of the island. The Elenan potters were contemporary with the Ostionan potters on the western half of Puerto Rico. Two ceramic styles for the

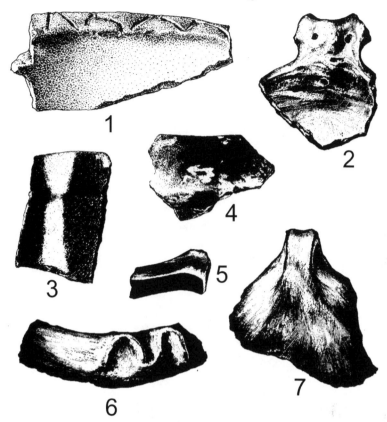

Figure 2.27. Ostionan Ostionoid pottery: *1*, red-slipped sherd from an outturned bowl with incision on a beveled rim; *2*, simply modeled head lug with a hole for suspension beneath it; *3*, red-painted design of vertical bands; *4*, red-slipped sherd from an inturned bowl; *5*, flipper from a red-slipped turtle-shaped bowl; *6*, sigmoid design modeled on a vessel shoulder; *7*, looped handle. (Reproduced from Rouse, *The Taínos*. Used by permission.)

Elenan subseries have been recognized in eastern Puerto Rico. The earliest is Monserrate (A.D. 600–850), and the other is Santa Elena (A.D. 850–1200). The major differences between the Monserrate and Cuevas styles are in vessel forms, with the latter characterized by WOR painting for most of the period. In the following Santa Elena period, ceramics are characterized by loss of strap handles, production of mainly bowl forms, the abandonment of painted decoration and polishing. Modeling and incising became the major ceramic decoration. As with the Ostionan subseries, the larger Elenan Ostionoid subseries sites have associated ball courts. Some sites, like Tibes, have multiple plazas and ball courts. Major sites associated with the Elenan Ostionoid subseries are Tibes, Collores, and El Bronce (Saunders 2005).

The Meillacan succeeded the Ostionan people in the Cibao valley of northern Hispaniola. About A.D. 800, the Meillacan people moved into Jamaica and Cuba, following the trail of their Ostiones forebears (Saunders 2005). The Meillacan people made unpainted pottery, often decorated with rectilinear incisions, crosshatched designs, punctuations, appliqué clay ridges, and small geometric and zoomorphic lugs (Saunders 2005). White Marl in Jamaica, which dates from A.D. 950 to 1500, is a major Meillacan Ostionoid and later Taíno site in the Greater Antilles. The White Marl Taino Midden and Museum is located on the Kingston to Spanish Town highway, adjacent to the White Marl Primary School. The museum, established in 1965 in memory of Randolph Howard, a distinguished American archaeologist, was built in the shape of a Taíno hut and forms part of the Amerindian Research Centre. The midden is considered the most valuable Taíno site in Jamaica and one of the most important in the Caribbean. Excavations of burial grounds on the White Marl hill have located remains of a number of fairly well-preserved adults and a child that predate Columbus's arrival by several centuries. Two other important Meillacan Ostionoid/Taíno sites are Stewart Castle and Retreat in north-central Jamaica. Contour and digital maps of both Stewart Castle and Retreat show the presence of mounds near or at the top of hills. In both cases, the dwellings of the villagers were arranged in an approximate circle with an open area (or plaza) in the middle (Figure 2.28). In the case of Retreat, the handmade contour map produced by Theodoor de Booy in 1913 shows the approximately eleven mounds more clearly when compared with the digital image of six mounds at Stewart Castle (Allsworth-Jones and Kappers 2007).

The Chican subseries, which had developed in Dominican Republic, spread to Puerto Rico and St. Croix, if not to the rest of the Virgin Islands, and strongly influenced the pottery of the northern Leewards (Rouse 1992). Bowls with incurving shoulders were now decorated with modeled-incised lugs and curvilinearly incised designs. They are defining characteristics of the late precolonial pottery on Anguilla and Saba (Douglas 1991; Hofman and Hoogland 1999). Usually associated with the Classic Taínos, Chican pottery, especially the Boca Chica style, is characterized by more highly polished surfaces and more refined modeled-incisions than the other Ostionoid pottery subseries elsewhere in the northern Caribbean (Rouse 1992). In various parts of Hispaniola, different pottery styles came into use. Meillacan potters were found primarily (though not exclusively) in the large interior valley of the north and in the western parts of Hispaniola while Chican potters were primarily in the southeast of the island. The relationship between Ostionan, Meillacan, and Chican potters was *not* a sequential one. The three related kinds of pottery were in use at the same time on various parts of Hispaniola (Wilson 1999).

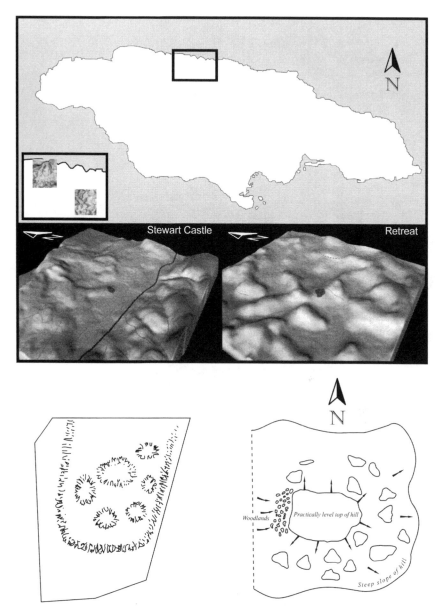

Figure 2.28. Digital maps of Meillacan Ostionoid/Taíno sites in Stewart Castle and Retreat, Jamaica, as well as a sketch plan of Stewart Castle (*bottom left*) by J. E. Duerden (1897) and a sketch plan of Retreat by Theodoor de Booy (1913).

Pottery made by the Lucayans of the Bahamas, called the Palmetto sub-series, can be found throughout both parts of the archipelago, the Turks and Caicos, and the Bahama Islands. Primarily because of the poor quality of the clay in the Bahamian archipelago, Palmetto potters made technologically inferior ceramics when compared to the rest of the Ostionoid pottery in the northern Caribbean (Rouse 1992). Thick, crude, and mostly shell-tempered, Palmetto pottery is so friable that it breaks into tiny sherds. Despite this, it shares some similarities with Meillacan pottery in appliqué work and punctuation (Rouse 1992).

The origins of the Ostionoids are still being debated. It was once assumed that all Ostionoids evolved from the Saladoids on Puerto Rico with possible influences from Archaic communities in eastern Hispaniola. However, new evidence indicates that the Ostionoids primarily evolved from Casimiroid (Archaic) peoples who had migrated from Central America to Cuba and Hispaniola. (See Chapter 4 for a fuller discussion of these issues.)

Conclusion

The presence of a variety of stone artifacts, pottery types, and other archaeological remains indicates that multiple groups either migrated into the Caribbean or evolved into new indigenous communities in the region. This information is important as it debunks the myth that the Arawaks and the Caribs were the two primary groups to have colonized the Caribbean. Rather than simplifying Caribbean history to accommodate the popular but false "peaceful Arawak/hostile Carib" dichotomy, students of history should be taught about the rich cultural diversity of the precolonial Antilles.

Myth 3

Columbus Met Arawaks in the Northern Caribbean

Generations of schoolchildren in the Anglophone Caribbean have been taught that the native peoples encountered by Christopher Columbus in Cuba, Hispaniola, Jamaica, Puerto Rico, and the Bahamas were Arawaks (Black 1983; Dookhan 2006; Ashdown and Humphreys 1988). However, archaeological and linguistic data indicate that the Amerindians who extensively settled in the northern Caribbean at the time of Spanish contact were very different from the peoples of South America whom we today call Arawaks.

~

It is impossible to write about the past without assigning names to the peoples about whom we write. Over the years a variety of names have been used to designate the precolonial peoples of the Americas. Unfortunately, the names that were selected have in some cases led to confusion regarding cultural heritage and ethnic identity. The name Arawak is one that has resulted in such significant confusion that archaeologists working in the region have now abandoned the name as it specifically relates to the Caribbean.

Origins of the Word *Arawak*

In order to recognize the substantial cultural differences between Arawak societies in mainland South America and the peoples of the northern Caribbean at the time of Spanish contact, Caribbean archaeologists now use the name Taínos in reference to the latter (Figure 3.1). This term relates specifically to natives who lived in the northern Caribbean from A.D. 1200 to 1500 and who had evolved from the Ostionoids. Although the names Taínos and Arawaks have been used interchangeably (Gilmore et al. 2003), from all accounts they were two distinct ethnic/cultural groups: the former located in northeastern

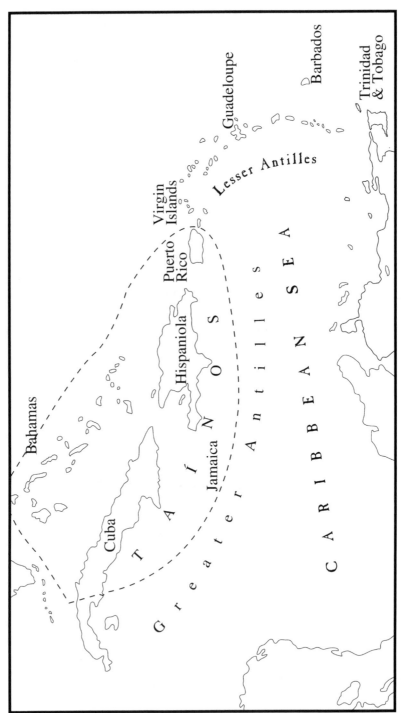

Figure 3.1. The Taínos in the Caribbean at the time of Spanish contact. (Adapted from Rouse, *The Taínos*. Used by permission.)

South America, while the latter occupied much of the Greater Antilles and the Bahamas at the time of Columbus. In fact, neither Columbus nor any of his contemporaries came across the word *Arawak* (Olsen 1974). Essentially, the word *Arawak* does not appear in the literature until the exploration of the Guianas began in the late 1500s, almost a century after the arrival of Columbus in the New World. Sir Walter Raleigh, the famed English explorer, identified the Arawaks and at least four other Indian groups when he visited Trinidad in 1595. Centuries later, in 1894, Juan Lopez de Velasco noted the presence of people who called themselves Arawaks on the Guiana coast, and commented that a group of them had "intruded" on Trinidad. The Arawaks of Trinidad have long ceased to be an identifiable ethnic group, although the Santa Rosa Carib community based in Arima, Trinidad, is purportedly the product of the mixing of several native groups, including the Arawaks. However, there are numerous Arawak villages in Guyana, Suriname, northern Brazil, and French Guiana to this day (Carlin and Arends 2002; Martijn Vandenbel 2007, personal communication).

In the past, some scholars have commented on certain linguistic similarities between these native peoples of South America and those encountered by Columbus in the northern Caribbean. In 1871, for instance, Daniel Brinton, after studying a few word lists that survived in the Greater Antilles with the modern language of the Arawaks in the Guianas, came to the conclusion that the Amerindians in the Greater Antilles also conversed in the language spoken by the Arawaks. He applied the name Island-Arawak to the Antilleans in order to distinguish them from the peoples of the mainland. Unfortunately, this distinction was lost and the peoples of the Caribbean came to be known simply as Arawaks (Carlin and Arends 2002; Vandenbel 2007, personal communication). Subsequent authors such as Sven Lovén (1935) have demonstrated a preference for Insular Arawak or the Island-Arawak (Reid 1994).

Linguistic and Cultural Differences between the Taínos and the Arawaks

The Taínos, who inhabited the northern Caribbean at contact, spoke a different language and were culturally distinct from the South American Arawaks. At a general level, the languages of the Taínos and the Arawaks share enough similarities to be classified as members of the Arawakan language family (Keegan 1992). However, this is not surprising as the languages of the Taínos, Arawaks, and Island-Caribs all originated from the Arawak family of languages, which extended from the Upper Amazon Basin to Venezuela, the Guianas, and the West Indies (Figure 3.2). But the differences between these languages were substantial and whatever similarities existed could be com-

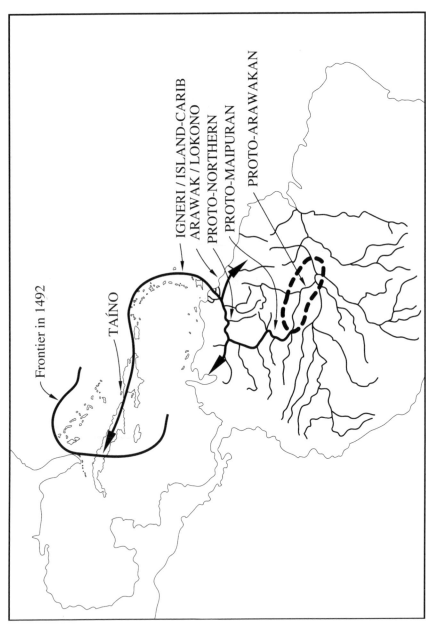

Frontier in 1492

TAÍNO

IGNERI / ISLAND-CARIB
ARAWAK / LOKONO
PROTO-NORTHERN
PROTO-MAIPURAN

PROTO-ARAWAKAN

Figure 3.2. Advance of the Arawakan speech-communities from Amazonia into the Caribbean. (Adapted from Rouse, *The Taínos.* Used by permission.)

pared to those between English and Dutch within the Indo-European family of languages (Olsen 1974; Reid 1994).

The Arawak language itself (now called Lokono) is better documented than that of the Taínos (Bennett 1989; Noble 1965; Rouse 1992). Many Taíno terms are known, but they refer mostly to localities, artifacts, and beliefs, all of which are considered unreliable because they could easily have been borrowed from neighboring languages (Rouse 1992). Linguists prefer to use basic vocabularies, that is, words expressing ideas that are common to all human beings and hence are not susceptible to foreign influence, such as the names for parts of the human body and for geographical features (Hock 1986). The number of cognates shared by a pair of languages is indicative of how long ago the two diverged from their common ancestor; the smaller the number, the earlier the time of divergence. There is general consensus among linguists that the Taíno, Island-Carib, and Arawak languages diverged from the main line of Arawak development at the same time and that all three belong to the Maipuran family. However, scholarly research (Noble 1965) has shown that the Taíno language shared few cognates with its nearest neighbors: Island-Caribs and Arawaks at the time of European contact. Therefore its line of development had branched off the trunk of the family tree earlier than the lines leading to the Island-Caribs and the Arawaks (Rouse 1992).

The cultural differences between the Taínos and the Arawaks clearly distinguished one group from the other. Although the Taínos and the Arawaks both worshipped ancestral spirits (*zemis*) and used griddles to bake cassava bread, archaeological and ethnohistorical data indicate that the latter had a simpler culture. While the Arawaks slashed and burned the forest to make temporary farms, the Taínos of the Caribbean, especially those in Hispaniola and Puerto Rico, practiced a sophisticated *conuco* agriculture, based on mounds of earth in more permanent fields. The mounds, 1 m (3 ft) high and some 2.7 m (9 ft) in circumference, were arranged in regular rows. They retarded erosion, improved drainage, and thus permitted more lengthy in-ground storage of root crops (Rouse 1992). In contrast to the Arawaks of South America, the Taínos built much larger, permanent villages. The latter were characterized by a more elaborate sociopolitical organization, with district and even regional chiefdoms as well as ballparks and plazas (Wilson 1990).

Controversy

However, the use of the word *Taíno* has not been without controversy. *Taíno* means "good" or "noble," and several of its members allegedly used that word to Columbus's crew to indicate that they were not Island-Caribs. This was documented in Peter Martyr d'Anghera's (1587) account of an incident during Columbus's second voyage while Melchior Maldonado was exploring the coast of Hispaniola:

> In the course of their exploration of this country, the Spaniards per- ceived in the distance a large house, which they approached, persuaded that it was the retreat of Guaccanarillo. They were met by a man with a wrinkled forehead and frowning brows, who was escorted by about a hundred warriors armed with bows and arrows, pointed lances and clubs. He advanced menacingly towards them, 'Taíno,' the natives cried, that is to say good men, not cannibals. In response to our amicable signs, they dropped their arms and modified their ferocious attitude (English translation in D'Anghera 1912 1:81; Spanish in Gil & Varela 1984:60). (Hulme 1993)

The validity of this account has been questioned (Hulme 1993), given that Peter Martyr was not an eyewitness to the event nor did he ever set foot in the New World. Moreover, naming a culture by a greeting is not logical at all. It is tantamount to saying "hello, culture," "good day, culture," "bienvenidos, cul- ture" and so on.

It has been argued that the word *Taíno* was first used, in an academic con- text, by Constantine Samuel Rafinesque in 1836. Rafinesque's MesoAmerican and Caribbean studies were centered on linguistic data, which he extracted from printed sources, mostly those of travelers. As an alternative to Island- Arawak (Hulme 1993), he used the term Taíno in specific reference to the lan- guage spoken anciently in Haiti. Over time, others (Wilson 1990; Rouse 1992) applied the word *Taíno* to the ethnicity of natives in the northern Caribbean at contact. The word *nitayno*, which bears a striking similarity to Taíno, has cropped up in the Spanish literature as referring to Taíno nobility (Rouse 1992). According to Columbus's diary entry for December 23, 1492, he had the fol- lowing encounters with the natives of Hispaniola: "All of the Indians returned with the Christians to the village, which he affirms to be the largest and best arranged with streets than any other passed through and found up to that time. . . . Until then the Admiral had not been able to understand whether the cacique meant King or governor. They also use another name for an important person, whom they call *nitayno*. He does not know if they say it for noble or governor or judge (Columbus 1989:271)" (Hulme 1993).

Rather than being used as an ethnic label, *nitayno* referred to the Taíno rul- ing class (Rouse 1992), which was probably a reflection of the natives being viewed through the prism of the Spanish class structure. It has even been pro- posed that the term Taíno should be altogether scrapped as an ethnic classifi- cation (Whitehead 1995) as it gives the erroneous impression that the northern

Caribbean was inhabited by a single, largely homogeneous culture (Keegan 1996a). One school of thought argues that the islanders whom Columbus encountered on his first voyage did not have a self-designation or if they did Columbus did not make mention of it. He simply called them *indios* (Whitehead 1995), as the Admiral mistakenly thought that he had "discovered" natives of islands off the coast of Asia.

Heterogeneity

Although there seemed to have been one dominant speech community, the Taínos were not a single, largely homogenous culture as the presence of several mutually unintelligible languages in Hispaniola at contact was first recorded by Bartolomé de Las Casas (Granberry 1993). Differences in physical appearance and material culture between the natives of northeastern Hispaniola and those elsewhere on the island were reported by Columbus (Dunn and Kelley 1989). Ramón Pané collected data on native religion in Macorix (Macorix means "foreign tongue" in the Taíno language), a small territory in Hispaniola with a unique language, yet the beliefs he recorded have been generalized to all Taínos (Rouse 1992; Keegan 1996a).

To further confound the issue, a number of subdivisions relating to both geography and cultural development are being used in Caribbean archaeology, namely Classic, Western, and Eastern Taínos (Figure 3.3). Taínos in Puerto Rico and Hispaniola, with the highest level of sociopolitical development (including ball courts, stone-lined plazas, and conucos) are called Classic Taínos by Caribbean archaeologists, while the less developed members of the Taíno community residing elsewhere in the northern Caribbean are referred to as Western and Eastern Taínos (Rouse 1992). Besides being called Western Taínos, the natives of the Bahamas have also come to be known as the Lucayans, which is an anglicized form of the Spanish name Las Islas de Los Lucayos (Keegan 1992). These names are more reflective of broad regional classifications rather than localized differences and represent an effort by some Caribbean archaeologists (Rouse 1992) to capture the level of indigenous plurality that existed at contact.

Whether or not the natives of the Greater Antilles and the Caribbean actually identified themselves as Taínos is still a subject of considerable debate. A number of archaeologists have suggested that the use of this name masks significant variability among the societies that have come to share this name. The fact that they belonged for the most part to a single speech community (Olsen 1974; Rouse 1987) is strongly suggestive of the presence of an ethnic grouping in the northern Caribbean, even if there is some uncertainty as to their self-designation. Spanish writers reported that the Amerindian inhabitants of the

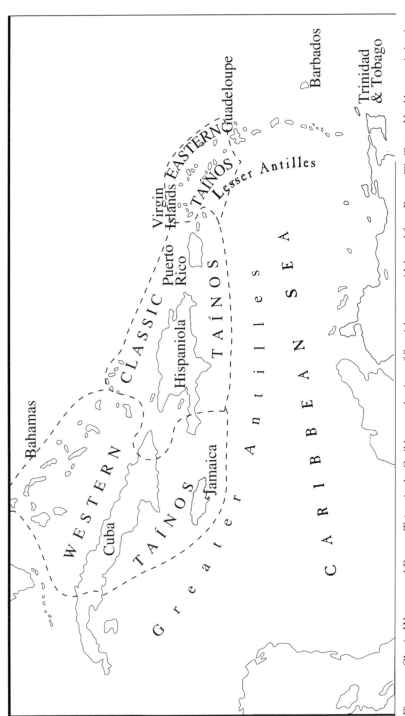

Figure 3.3. Classic, Western, and Eastern Taínos in the Caribbean at the time of Spanish contact. (Adapted from Rouse, *The Taínos*. Used by permission.)

Greater Antilles and the Bahamas spoke a single language, and Columbus was able to use the same interpreter almost everywhere he went (Olsen 1974; Rouse 1987). For example, in referring to Puerto Rico, Hispaniola, Cuba, and Jamaica, Bartolomé de Las Casas, primary sixteenth-century chronicler of the Indies, reiterated many times in his epochal *Historia de las Indias* that "en todas estas islas hablaban una sola lengua" (in all these islands they speak a single language) (Granberry and Vescelius 2004). Yet Las Casas and other writers of the early 1500s clearly distinguished a number of other aboriginal languages in the Greater Antilles such as Macorix, Ciguayo, and Guanahatabey. The most reasonable explanation for this is that the Taíno language of the Greater Antilles, which had many monolingual speakers and was the numerically dominant language of the Greater Antilles, also served as a language of interchange, even with the speakers of other languages, serving much the same purpose and for essentially the same reasons as Norman French in post-1066 England (Granberry and Vescelius 2004). In addition to being the native language of many, it was essentially a lingua franca.

Language uniformity does not necessarily reflect the presence of an ethnic group; a single speech community may be the result of colonization or assimilation. Although the Carib peoples of South America speak a Cariban language, while the Caribs of the Windward Islands speak an Arawakan language, the latter are also called Caribs, although the preferred ascriptions are Island-Caribs (Rouse 1992), Kalina (Rouse 1992), and Kalinagos (Beckles 1992). English has been the official language of the Anglo-Caribbean for centuries because of British colonial rule. However, the extensive use of English belies the many ethnic and cultural differences that exist in specific territories within the region. In Trinidad and Tobago, for example, people of East Indian, African, Chinese, and Lebanese descent all speak English. Furthermore, the fact that English is the official language of communication of the twin island republic does not make its speakers British.

Conclusion

Despite the controversy surrounding the word *Taíno,* it is generally accepted that there were significant linguistic and cultural differences between the contact-period natives of the northern Caribbean on the one hand and the Arawaks of South America on the other hand. On this basis, it would be grossly inaccurate to refer to the inhabitants of the Greater Antilles and the Bahamas at the time of Spanish contact as Arawaks. The jury is still out on whether the word *Taíno* is entirely accurate as it is presently used. Suffice it to say that Caribbean archaeologists will continue to use it until they find a better alternative.

Myth 4

The Natives Encountered by Christopher Columbus in the Northern Caribbean Migrated from South America

Over the years, the impression has been given that the natives living in the northern Caribbean at the time of contact were in fact migrants from South America. However, archaeological data indicate that these groups were a Caribbean phenomenon as they were well established centuries before Columbus's arrival and evolved autochthonously or indigenously in the region. The Taínos in Cuba and Hispaniola were the result of the pottery-making Casimiroids evolving into Ostionoids, who later became Taínos. On the other hand, the Taínos in Puerto Rico were the product of cultural interactions between the Saladoids in western Puerto Rico and Casimiroids in eastern Hispaniola.

~

A number of history books continue to perpetuate the misconception that the native peoples whom Columbus met in the northern Caribbean migrated from South America. For example, "The aborigines, or earliest inhabitants, of Jamaica, of whom we have definite records were the Arawak Indians, also called Tainans. Originating in the region of the Guianas and Venezuela where Arawaks are still to be found, these people at some very distant time sailed northward in their dug-out canoes, settling in each of the islands of the Antilles, from Trinidad to Cuba, arriving in Jamaica around A.D. 1000" (Black 1983). A later publication (Gilmore 2003) bears a similar perspective: "The Tainos arrived from between the first and 7th centuries CE [common era], and moved northwards throughout the Lesser Antilles until they finally settled in the islands of the Greater Antilles." However, archaeological evidence has established that the Taínos were well established in the northern Caribbean from A.D. 1200 to A.D. 1500 (Wilson 1997) and therefore did not migrate from South America. In other words, they developed autochthonously or indigenously in the Caribbean over several generations, similar to the local development of East Indian, African, Chinese, Lebanese descendants or any other ethnic group in a variety of Caribbean territories such as Trinidad and Tobago, Jamaica, Barbados, St. Lucia, Grenada and Guyana. There are three schools of thought with respect to Taíno genesis in the northern Caribbean.

The Saladoid-Archaic-Ostionoid-Taíno Model

The first school of thought, described here as the Saladoid-Archaic-Ostionoid-Taíno model, argues that the Taínos evolved out of interactions between the Saladoid and Casimiroid (Archaic) peoples. According to this theory, the Saladoids migrated from South America, reached Puerto Rico about 500 B.C. and stalled in Puerto Rico for about 1,000 years. As a result, pottery was not introduced to the rest of the Greater Antilles until much later. The Saladoids in Puerto Rico were unable to move beyond the eastern tip of Hispaniola for 1,000 years because of the presence of relatively large, well-established Casimiroid descendants in Hispaniola. During this period, the relationship changed and the archaeological record suggests that there were intense cultural interactions between the two groups, leading to the creation of a new cultural entity—the Ostionoids. The process is best described as transculturation. Coined by Fernando Ortiz in 1947, transculturation can be defined as the constant interaction between two or more cultural components with the unconscious goal of creating a third cultural identity.

The discovery of a crude pottery, known as El Caimito (Figure 4.1), at the La Caleta site in eastern Dominican Republic has been interpreted as evidence for interactions between the Casimiroid peoples of eastern Hispaniola and the Saladoid colonists of Puerto Rico (Rouse 1992). The site is radiocarbon dated at 305 B.C. to A.D. 120 and contains Archaic tool types (Keegan 1994). According to this model, the pottery vessels and designs of the Saladoids were simplified during the 1,000 year pause in Puerto Rico. For example, the distinctive characteristic of Saladoid pottery—the elaborate white-on-red painting—was abandoned in favor of simpler decorative styles. The assumption is that the Ostionoid culture, which developed out of Saladoid and Casimiroid interactions at eastern Hispaniola/western Puerto Rico interface, spread east, west, and north to the other islands by A.D. 600, eventually leading to the emergence of the Taínos in the Greater Antilles (Figures 4.2–4.4).

The Archaic-Ostionoid-Taíno Model

The second school of thought, which is based on more current research, seriously challenges the notion that the Ostionoids and later the Taínos evolved out of interactions between the Saladoid and the Archaic peoples (with the geographical center of this transculturation being the interface between west-

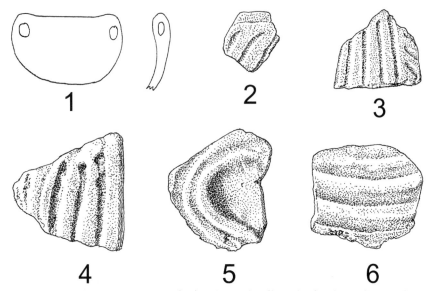

Figure 4.1. El Caimito pottery: *1*, bowl (*left*) with strap handle; *2*, sherd with curvilinear incision; *3*, sherd with rectilinear incision; *4*, sherd with lines ending in punctuations; *5*, sherd with modeling; *6*, sherd with curvilinear incision. (Reproduced from Rouse, *The Taínos*. Used by permission.)

ern Puerto Rico and eastern Hispaniola). This theory argues that pottery was in fact being produced by the Casimiroid peoples of Cuba and Hispaniola and their descendants about 2,000 years before the arrival of the Saladoids in the Caribbean, and by Ortoiroid peoples in the Lesser Antilles and Puerto Rico before the Ostionoid expansion. The theory further argues that the pottery-making Casimiroid descendants in both Cuba and Hispaniola evolved into Ostionoids, with the Ostionoids on these islands subsequently colonizing neighboring Caribbean territories (Figures 4.5–4.8).

There is considerable evidence for pottery-making by Archaic peoples in the Caribbean. In Haiti, there is pottery at the Archaic Couri I site (Rouse 1941). As far back as 1921, mention was being made of pottery in Archaic sites in Cuba (Harrington 1921). Twelve Archaic sites in Cuba bearing pottery were identified in the 1980s (Dacal Moure and Rivero de la Calle 1984). In the Dominican Republic, besides El Caimito (La Caleta) and Musié Pedro sites, which date to as early as 300 B.C. (Veloz, Ortega, and Pina 1974; Veloz et al. 1976), similar sites have been found at Honduras del Oeste and El Barrio (Rímoli and Nadal 1980). Pottery at Archaic sites on Puerto Rico was reported for Playa Blanca and Jobos (Rouse 1952). This wide distribution of pottery in Archaic sites prior to the arrival of the Saladoids indicates that pottery was not

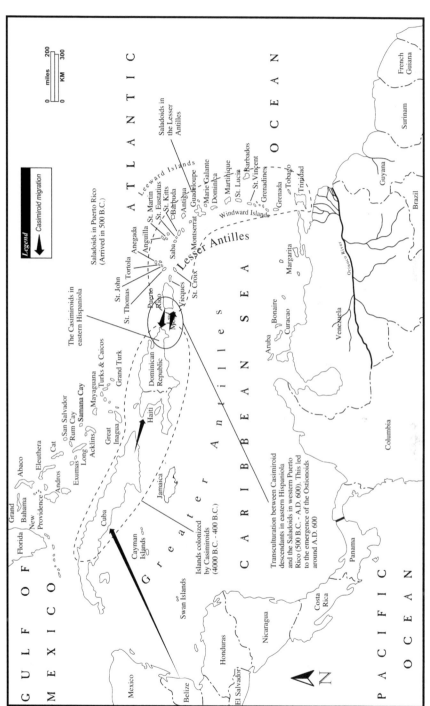

Figure 4.2. The Saladoid–Archaic–Ostionoid–Taíno model.

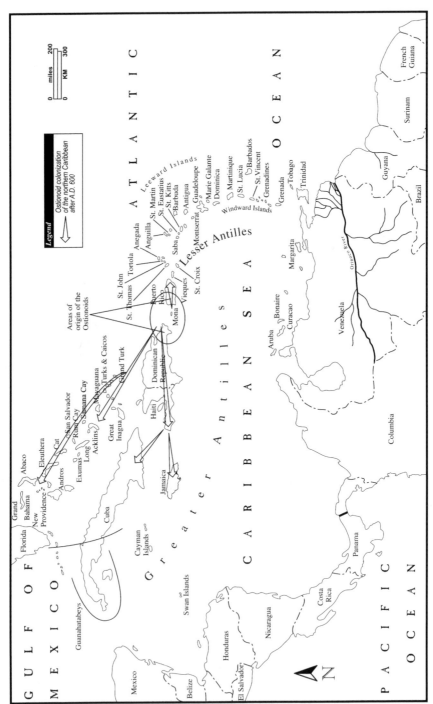

Figure 4.3: The Saladoid-Archaic-Ostionoid-Taíno model.

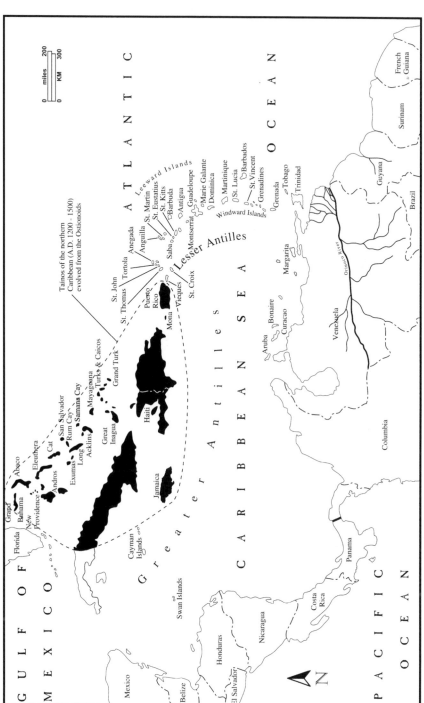

Figure 4.4 The Saladoid–Archaic–Ostionoid–Taíno model.

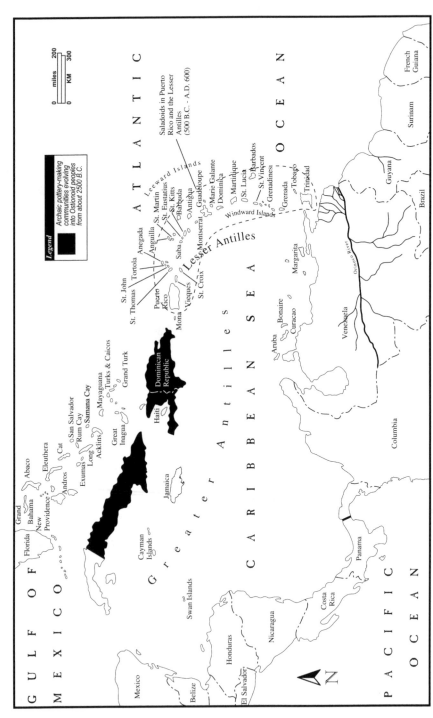

Figures 4-5. The Archaic-Ostionoid-Taíno model.

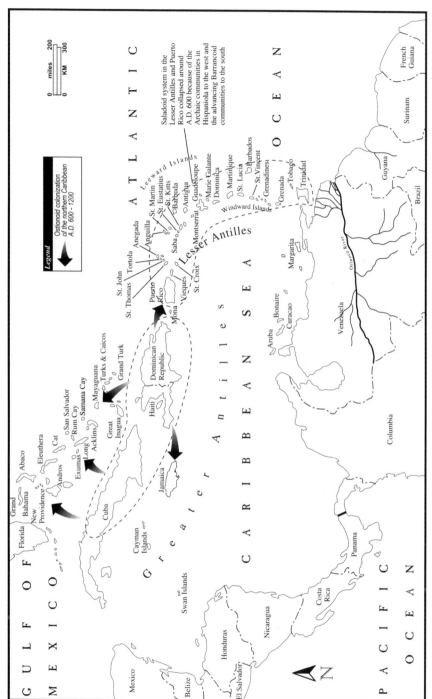

Figure 4.6. The Archaic-Ostionoid-Taíno model.

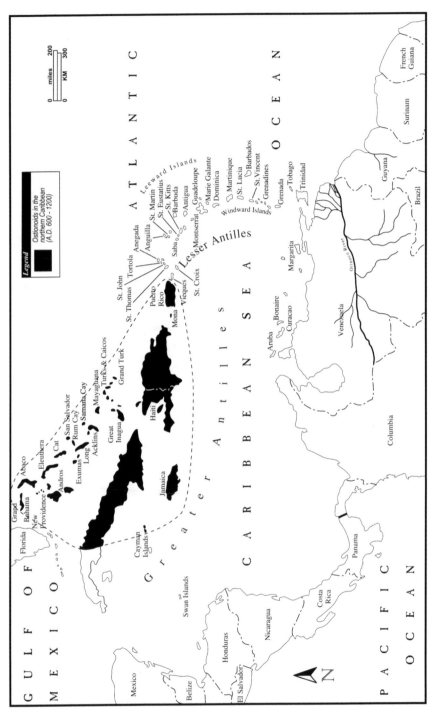

Figure 4.7. The Archaic-Ostionoid-Taíno model.

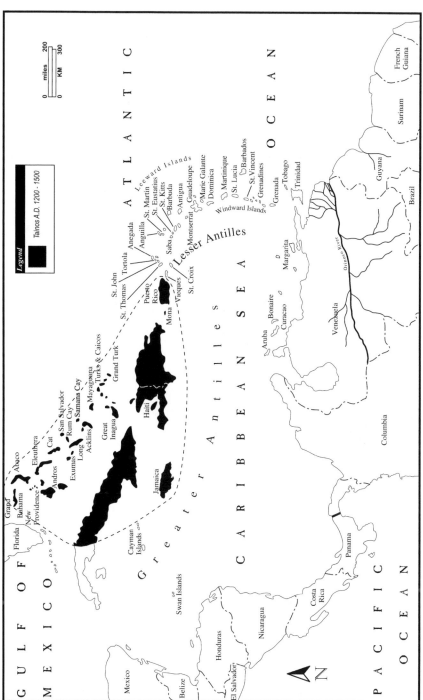

Figure 4.8. The Archaic-Ostionoid-Taíno model.

introduced to the Greater Antilles by Saladoid colonists (Keegan and Rodríguez Ramos 2007).

The features of the late Archaic ceramics of Haiti, Hispaniola, and Puerto Rico bear a strong resemblance to early Ostionoid pottery but also reflect a period of experimentation where different pastes and different decorative techniques were explored (Jouravleva 2002; Keegan and Rodríguez Ramos 2007). Sherds are not common at these sites, and they exhibit a high degree of variability. Despite this, there are some general patterns, namely globular bowls, with round or flat bottoms, and boat-shaped are the main vessel forms. Red, pink, white or black paint along with incised and modeled designs are the most common decorations. In addition, the flaked-stone artifacts and shell-tools on Ostionoid sites look more similar to Archaic artifacts than tools found in Saladoid sites. These cultural similarities suggest that the Ostionoid people, who later became the Taínos, may have in fact evolved from the Archaic peoples rather than the Saladoids. The extensive Archaic presence in the Greater Antilles, which later gave rise to the Ostionoids, probably explains the rapid expansion of the latter across Hispaniola, Cuba and Jamaica and the Bahamas after A.D. 700 when they seemed to have been stuck in Puerto Rico/eastern Hispaniola for 1,000 years, if we are to subscribe to the Saladoid-Archaic-Ostionoid-Taíno model.

The Archaic-Saladoid-La Hueca-Ostionoid-Taíno Model

Though important, the Archaic-Saladoid-La Hueca-Ostionoid-Taíno model has generally received insufficient attention in Caribbean archaeology (Curet 2005; Chanlatte Baik 1986). The model does not assume that the Archaic peoples or cultures were eradicated from Puerto Rico once the Saladoid-La Hueca people arrived on the island. On the contrary, it proposes that they came in contact with each other and established a relationship that lasted for some time. Two main Ostionoid subseries, Ostionan Ostionoid and Elenan Ostionoid, emerged as products of this period of cultural interactions between the Archaic and Saladoid-La Hueca peoples (Curet 2005). The Ostionan subseries developed from interactions between the Saladoid and Archaic groups, while the Elenan subseries arose from contacts between La Hueca and the Archaic groups (Curet 2005). Shortly after their emergence, the Ostionoids in Puerto Rico quickly colonized neighboring islands in the northern Caribbean, evolving into Taínos by A.D. 1200 (Figures 4.9–4.13). There is some archaeological evidence from Ostionoid deposits in Puerto Rico that supports this model. While large amounts of seashells, characteristic of many Archaic deposits, have been found in Ostionoid deposits in Puerto Rico, far less quantities of seashells have been identified in Saladoid-La Hueca assemblages (Curet 2005).

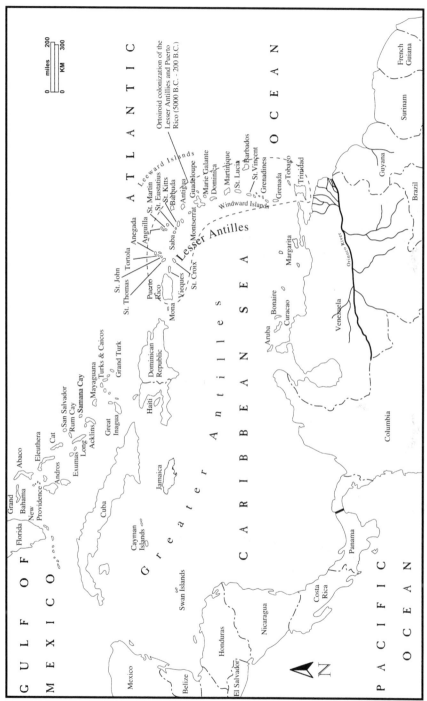

Figure 4.9. The Archaic–Saladoid–La Hueca–Ostionoid–Taíno model.

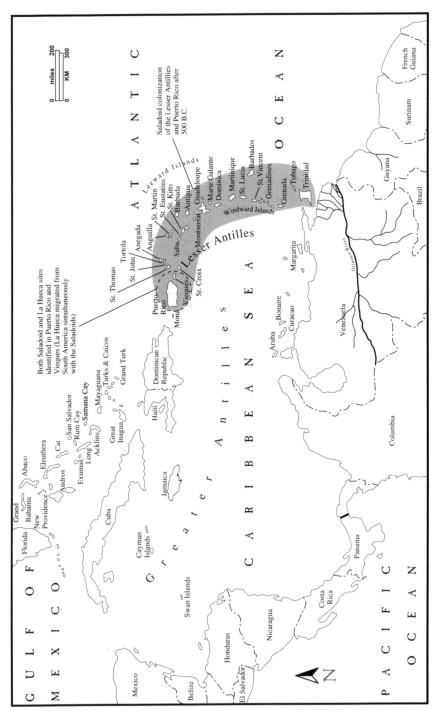

Figure 4.10. The Archaic-Saladoid-La Hueca-Ostionoid-Taíno model.

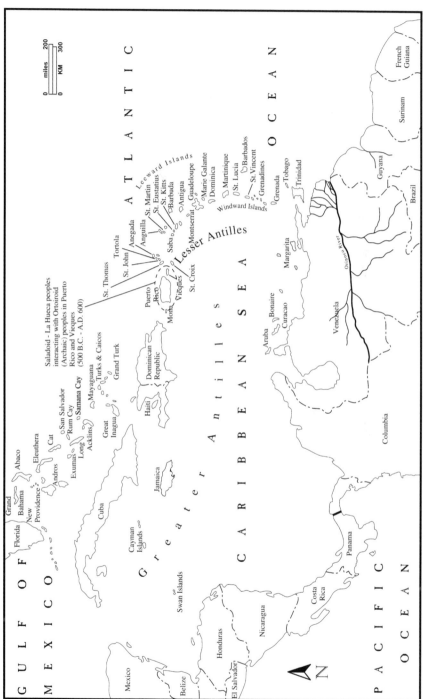

Figure 4.11. The Archaic-Saladoid-La Hueca-Ostionoid-Taíno model.

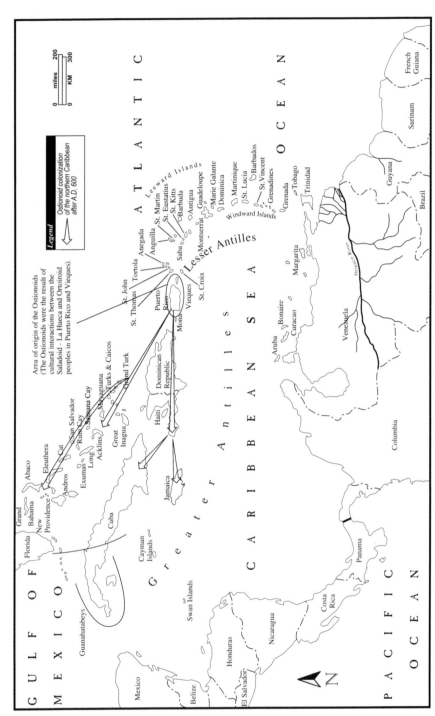

Figure 4.12. The Archaic-Saladoid-La Hueca-Ostionoid-Taíno model.

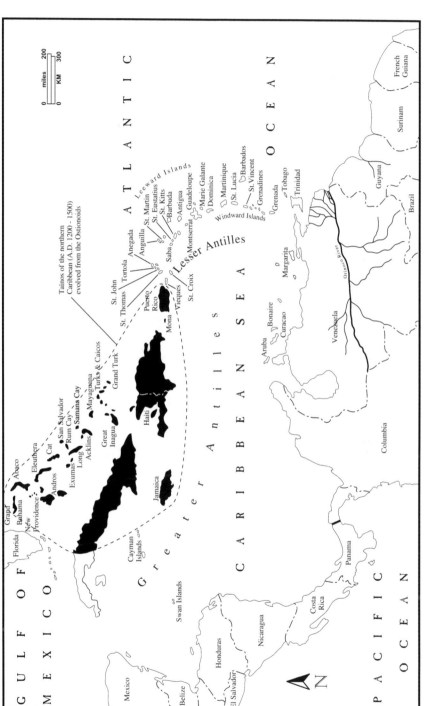

Figure 4.13. The Archaic-Saladoid-La Hueca-Ostionoid-Taíno model.

It is also significant that there are more similarities between the lithic technology of the Ostionoids in Puerto Rico and their Archaic forerunners vis-à-vis the stone technology practiced by the Saladoid-La Hueca (Rodríguez Ramos 2002a, 2002b). A major shortcoming of the Archaic-Saladoid-La Hueca-Ostionoid-Taíno model is that it was presented in very general terms by its originator (Chanlatte Baik 1986) without any specific details being given on the dynamics of Saladoid-La Hueca-Archaic interactions (Curet 2005). More intensive research should therefore be invested in explaining this aspect of the model.

The Taínos Developed Locally in the Caribbean

The evidence more strongly supports the Archaic-Ostionoid-Taíno model, at least for Cuba and Hispaniola. On the other hand, the Taínos in western Puerto Rico appeared to have been a product of cultural interactions between the Saladoids in Puerto Rico and Casimiroids in eastern Hispaniola. The Archaic-Saladoid-La Hueca-Ostionoid-Taíno model is also plausible for explaining Ostionoid origins in Puerto Rico. Although the three models propose different geographical zones as areas of Ostionoid origins in the northern Caribbean, there is general consensus that the Ostionoids who subsequently gave rise to the Taínos developed locally in the region.

Conclusion

Essentially, the Taínos did not migrate from South America but evolved indigenously in the Caribbean, emerging around A.D. 1200 as a product of distinct types of ancestral societies and multiple historical processes (Keegan and Rodríguez Ramos 2007). In Puerto Rico, the Taínos reflected the syncretism of the Saladoid-La Hueca and the Archaic-influenced Ostionoid, while in Hispaniola and Cuba, the Taínos had stronger ties to Casimiroid (Archaic) traditions (Keegan and Rodríguez Ramos 2007). The Taínos played the same ball game as their predecessors; their settlements were similar, although larger and more numerous; and their religious beliefs and rituals were related to their Saladoid, Archaic (Wilson 1997), and Ostionoid forerunners.

Myth 5

The Arawaks Were the First Potters and Farmers to Have Settled in the Caribbean

While some scholars use the term *Arawak* in reference to this first migratory wave of pottery-making, agriculturalists into the Caribbean (Rogonzinki 2000; Ashdown and Humphreys 1988), the term is fraught with controversy (see Chapter 3). Moreover, it does not accurately reflect the diversity of Ceramic-age, horticultural groups arriving in the region from 5000 B.C. to 1492 (see Chapter 2). Until recently, there was general agreement among Caribbean archaeologists that the Saladoids were the first potters and farmers. However, there is mounting evidence that the Ortoiroids and Casimiroids, who had arrived in the Caribbean about 5000 B.C. and 4000 B.C., respectively, were actually the first potters and farmers in the Antilles.

～

Were the Saladoids First?

The term *Arawak* is a misnomer for the northern Caribbean and is more applicable for describing certain native groups in South America (see Chapter 3). This dispels any notion that the Arawaks were the first potters and farmers in the Antilles. Until recently, there was general agreement among Caribbean archaeologists (Wilson 1990; Rouse 1992; Keegan 2000) that the Saladoids were the first horticultural, Ceramic-age group. Saladoid sites are found in abundance from Trinidad and Tobago to Puerto Rico and with their arrival in 500 B.C. came visible signs of their South American farming background, such as ceramic pots and cassava griddles, as well as physical evidence of a settled village life, such as large middens and plazas. However, the idea that Saladoids introduced pottery and agriculture to the islands is based on outdated models of cultural development and migration. New evidence indicates that pottery-making and agriculture were already practiced in the islands by both the Casimiroid and Ortoiroid peoples at least two thousand years before the Saladoids arrived.

Archaic Potters

The discovery of crude pottery, known as El Caimito, at the La Caleta site in the eastern Dominican Republic was initially interpreted as evidence for trans-culturation between the Casimiroids of eastern Hispaniola and the Saladoids of western Puerto Rico (Keegan 1994). However, the ongoing discovery of a significant number of Casimiroid and Ortoiroid pottery-bearing sites points to the Archaic inhabitants, not the Saladoids, as the first potters and farmers in the region (Figure 5.1) (Hung 2005). To date, no Archaic sites have been found in Jamaica, but this may be a result of the island being underresearched.

Regional Trends

Rather than interpreting Archaic pottery-making and horticulture in the Caribbean region as isolated phenomena, they should be viewed as part of a much larger emerging trend in the circum-Caribbean and New World tropics. The Caribbean coast of Colombia is one of those areas where evidence of early pottery has been reported. Shell middens such as Puerto Hormiga (3150–2550 B.C.) and San Jacinto (4000 B.C.) (Angulo 1992; Ford 1969; Scott et al. 1991; Veloz Maggiolo 1991) and the contemporaneous Monsú, seem to demonstrate the first attempts of village life in the region (Hung 2005). Their general characteristics suggest a transition from incipient agricultural practices and intensive gathering to a reliance on cultivated tubers such as manioc. This seems to be the case at other Colombian sites, such as Rotinet and Malambo, where the consumption of manioc in the form of cassava became habitual around 2000 and 1200 B.C., respectively (Angulo 1992; Hung 2005). Sites studied in the region of Carúpano in Venezuela (Sanoja 1988; Vargas 1987) provide significant examples of the development reached by the foraging groups from this region of South America. These sites consist of large shell middens with surface ceramics and a mixed economy. The foragers of this area of Venezuela settled coastal areas near mangroves and lagoons in the gulfs of Paria and Cariaco (Hung 2005). In Guyana, on the other hand, studies of late phases of the Archaic groups associated with shell middens (such as Hosororo Creek, 2025 B.C.) document how communities with a basic gathering economy developed an undecorated pottery with very simple forms (Hung 2005; Williams 1992). In Central America, some shell middens, such as Monagrillo (2550–1250 B.C.) located in the Gulf of Panama, show evidence of a certain ceramic industry related to the use and exploitation of nearby resources in the man-

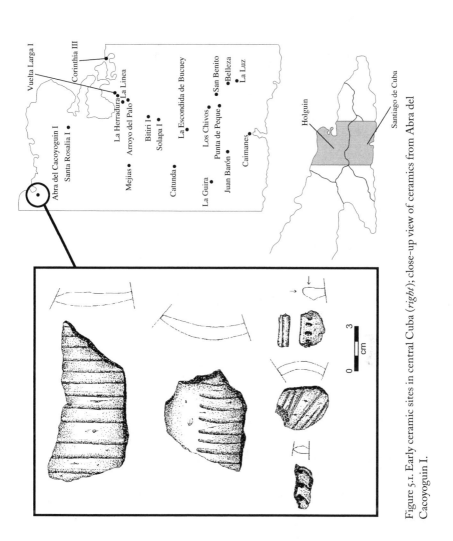

Figure 5.1. Early ceramic sites in central Cuba (*right*); close-up view of ceramics from Abra del Cacoyoguin I.

grove swamp. The pottery at this site gives the impression that this location was home to an important phase in the dispersion and exchange of ceramic traditions in the Americas.

In general, the shell middens with ceramics from Colombia, the coast of Venezuela, Guyana, and Panama reflect a phase of growth and intensification of foraging lifeways in the continental or riverine Caribbean, characterized by experimentation with some horticultural practices and the manufacturing of wood-working instruments and tools (Hung 2005). Assemblages of simple pottery appear to be correlated with an increase in site size and the production of grinding tools. All this appears to be in agreement with the transformations that took place in the economy of foraging societies, in which the consumption of vegetable foods shifted from marginal importance to become a central production process (Curet et al. 2005).

Definitions

Despite these trends, referring to both of the Ortoiroids and Casimiroids of the Caribbean as well as the Archaic peoples of the New World tropics as farmers raises the important issue of what constitutes farming. Also called agriculture, farming has been defined in a variety of ways: the practice of cultivating the land or raising stock; production that relies essentially on the growth and nurturing of plants and animals, especially for food, usually with land as an important input; and the science or process of cultivating the soil for the production of plants and animals that will be useful to humans in some way. Horticulture, which derives from the Latin *hortus,* meaning a "garden" space, in contrast to an "agricultural" space, is usually defined as the science and art of growing fruit, flowers, ornamental plants, and vegetables in small gardens. However, the archaeological literature has increasingly presented agriculture and horticulture as synonymous activities (Foster 2003; Cauchois 2002; Lee and Daly 2004).

Another complicating factor is that many societies have either shifted back and forth from foraging to farming as conditions allowed or have been characterized by a mixed economy based on foraging, farming, and fishing (Bogucki 1999). For instance, the Agta in the Philippines, long thought to be the prototypical hunter-gatherers (Peterson 1978a, 1978b), actually are opportunists who make use of the subsistence strategy that best suits the conditions of the moment (Griffin 1984). Food-producing populations have often lived in proximity to groups for whom farming and herding had little importance. Even among populations that were fully committed to agriculture, such as those of medieval and early Europe, gathered foods played an important role in the diet (Bogucki 1999).

Ingold (1984:5) has noted that anthropologists have the tendency to remove people from the category of foragers if they have any attributes of agriculture or pastoralism. There are really, however, three categories and two subcategories of human groups in terms of subsistence systems:

1. those who subsist on uncultivated plants and wild fauna—foragers
2. those who have a mixed subsistence economy, based partly on domestic and partly on wild resources
2a. foragers who farm (but are closer to category 1)
2b. farmers who hunt (but are closer to category 3)
3. those who gain no significant subsistence from uncultivated plants and wild fauna—agriculturalists and pastoralists

In general, anthropologists have tended to view the universe of human subsistence economies as a binary set: those in category 1 and those in category 3 (Bogucki 1999). The root of the problem may be that the colonization of Africa, the Americas, Australia, and the Pacific in the eighteenth and nineteenth centuries essentially "froze" many societies as either foragers or food producers, depending on their circumstances at the time of European contact. The point of this frozen moment was then assumed to be fixed on the unilinear scale of progress from hunting and gathering to farming and stock-herding (Bogucki 1999). Early ceramic societies in Cuba have been described as protoagricultural, which defines both a culture and a transitional stage (Tabío 1984). In this transitional phase between the preagricultural and agricultural stages, in addition to having an assemblage similar to that of the preagriculturalists, some Cuban aboriginal communities are distinguished by having evidence of ceramic vessel use, almost always simple and scarce in number, but without the presence of the burén (cassava griddle), indirect evidence of manioc agriculture (Tabío 1984). Despite the welter of definitions, what is clear is that the Archaic peoples of the Caribbean can properly be described as farmers, even though agriculture was in fact part of a larger network of other food-getting strategies such as collecting, fishing, and hunting.

Archaic Farmers

Inasmuch as hunter-gatherers in the eastern woodlands of the United States cultivated a number of local plants comprising the eastern agricultural complex, a similar Caribbean agricultural complex may have characterized the Archaic peoples of the region (Keegan 1987, 1994). The presence of certain plant remains on Archaic sites suggests that many of the foods, allegedly introduced by the Saladoids, were already an established part of Archaic horticulture

Figure 5.2. Palms (*Prestoea pubigera*).

(Newson 1993). Plants identified in Archaic deposits include zamia or coontie (*Zamia debilis*) and cupey (*Clusea rosea*) (Veloz Maggiolo and Vega 1982), wild avocado (*Persea Americana*) and yellow sapote (*Pouteria campechiana*) (Rouse and Alegría 1990), primrose (*Oenothera* sp.), mastic-bully (*Mastichodendron foetidissimum*), trianthema (*Trianthema portulaca*), and palms (Palmae) (Figure 5.2) (Newson 1993; Keegan 1994). Evidence for the use of palms such as corozo has been found in the macrobotanical (Newson 1993) and microbotanical record (Pagán Jiménez et al. 2005) of Puerto Rico. Starch grain analysis of Archaic edge-ground cobbles from Puerto Ferro in Puerto Rico showed many similarities with cobbles from early sites in the Isthmo-Colombian area that had been used for processing tubers such as manioc (*Manihot esculenta*), sweet potatoes (*Ipomoea batatas*), and tannia (*Xanthosoma* sp.) (Reniel Rodríguez 2007). This suggests that the Archaic peoples in Puerto Rico may have used their ground stone tools in a similar manner and that these plants were part and parcel of Archaic horticulture on the island.

Figure 5.3. Sapodilla (*Sapotaceae*).

In Dominican Republic, the site of El Caimito, interpreted as a food preparation area, is located on the roof of a rock shelter and is characterized by the presence of highly fragmented ceramics in small quantities (Hung 2005). Pollen analyses conducted on samples from El Caimito midden produced no evidence of cultivation of plants, such as manioc and corn, known to be used by the Saladoids, Ostionoids, and Taínos. Instead, pollen evidence points to intensive foraging based on the exploitation of *Zamia* sp., palm seeds (*Roystonea* sp.), and corozo (*Acrocomia* sp.) (Hung 2005). Fruit trees in the sapodilla family (Sapotaceae) (Figure 5.3) are represented by seeds and wood fragments from Twenty Hill on Antigua, and by seed remains from Hichmans' Shell Head, Nevis (Newson and Wing 2004:84). Other seeds from Archaic-age sites derive from herbaceous or slightly woody plants. Seeds that are provisionally assigned to the genus *Siphonoglossa* sp (Acanthaceae), cossie balsam, were recovered from Hichmans' Shell Heap in Nevis. This plant is documented among the floras of the northern Lesser Antilles, though apparently it is not recorded as part of the modern vegetation of Nevis (Howard 1989:372–73; Newson and

Wing 2004:86). Its archaeological presence suggests that this plant was utilized by the Ortoiroids of Nevis, resulting in its occurrence on the island. Cossie balsam is potentially another species that had medicinal value (Acevedo-Rodríguez 1996:50). Because some of these seeds were introduced from outside the Caribbean, and others have extensions beyond their present ranges, it is likely that at least some of these plants were managed if not cultivated outright (Newson 1993; Keegan 1994).

The Ortoiroids and the Casimiroids had migrated from northern South America and Belize in Central America, respectively—two lowland forested zones in the Americas where agriculture was developing independently from the beginning of the Holocene about 12,000 years ago (Piperno and Pearsall 1998). Agriculture evolved slowly in the region under consideration as a consequence of the persistence of low human population densities and the low level of social complexity that characterized early foragers even as they began to practice ever more sophisticated forms of plant management (Piperno and Pearsall 1998). Given their prior horticultural exposure on the mainland, it is conceivable that before and after migrating to the Caribbean from the mainland, these two Archaic groups were engaged in some measure of plant manipulation and domestication, although their subsistence was also heavily based on fishing, hunting, and mollusk (shell) collecting. This explains why many of the early plant cultivars found in the Greater and Lesser Antilles were also found extensively in Archaic contexts in northern South America and Central America (Newson and Pearsall 2003; Rodríguez Ramos 2007).

Conclusion

Although the Saladoids, Ostionoids, and Taínos practiced pottery-making and agriculture far more extensively than their Archaic forerunners (Newson and Wing 2004), the latter deserve credit for introducing both ceramic technology and farming to the Caribbean. In many ways, the Casimiroids and Ortoiroids laid the sociotechnological foundations for native societies that subsequently migrated to the Caribbean or developed indigenously or autochthonously in the region.

The Ciboneys Lived in Western Cuba at the Time of Spanish Contact

History books (Black 1983; Wilson 1990) and some archaeology texts (Rouse 1992; Dacal Moure and Rivero de la Calle 1997) refer to Ciboneys as a native group inhabiting western Cuba at the time of Spanish contact. The term is also used with respect to Archaic groups throughout the Caribbean. However, on both counts, the term Ciboneys is misapplied, as it actually refers to a local Taíno group in central Cuba. Guanahatabeys, not Ciboneys, is now the preferred term for native inhabitants of westernmost Cuba at contact. Even then, several questions remain about the actual existence of this group, with some arguing that it was probably a figment of the Spanish or Taíno imagination.

～

Because several history and archaeology books assert that the Ciboneys lived in western Cuba at contact, no wonder teachers and students often accept the notion. A variety of descriptions relating to Ciboney cultural traditions have been advanced (Dacal Moure and Rivero de la Calle 1997). For example, according to Black (1983): "In Haiti, Cuba and possibly Jamaica the Arawaks found an even more primitive tribe than themselves called Siboneys or 'rock-dwellers.' These people who had made their way down from Florida, were a simple fisher-folk. They lived mostly on the sea coast, made crude shell implements and, it is said, were used as servants by the Arawaks."

A later publication (Dacal Moure and Rivero de la Calle 1997) describes the Ciboneys as "the original settlers" of Cuba who had been largely replaced by the Taínos by the time of Columbus. It has been argued that these people had been pushed westward or absorbed by the encroaching Taínos and that they still lived on the southwestern Guacayarima peninsula of Hispaniola and the western end of Cuba when the Europeans arrived (Rouse 1992). Interestingly, Ciboneys have also been geographically placed in Florida and the Bahamas (Claypole and Robottom 2006), southwestern Hispaniola (Rouse 1992;

Gilmore et al. 2003), and the U.S. Virgin Islands. Hung (2005) claimed that the term was allegedly coined by early Spanish chronicles for hunter-gatherer groups and later developed as an archaeological cultural term by the North American investigator Mark R. Harrington.

The Term Ciboney Misapplied

Whether the presence of Ciboneys in Cuba was based on factual information or was a figment of Spanish or Taíno imagination continues to be debated in Caribbean archaeology. In the first instance, the term Ciboney, as applied to the natives in western Cuba and elsewhere in the Caribbean, is a misnomer as the term actually applies to a local Taíno group in central Cuba (Alegría 1981) and not to Archaic groups found throughout the Caribbean and circum-Caribbean, despite its continued use in this regard.

Guanahatabeys

The more generally accepted name used by Caribbean archaeologists for inhabitants of western Cuba at contact is Guanahatabeys (Figure 6.1) (Rouse 1992; Wilson 1990; Keegan 1992). Taíno inhabitants of Cuba who met the Spanish colonizers apparently mentioned some non-Taíno people called the Guanahatabeys or the Guanahacabibes. The Guanahatabeys were first described by Diego Velázquez de Cuéllar: "The life of these people is of the manner of savages, for they have neither houses or village quarters, nor field, nor do they eat anything else but the flesh they take in the mountains and turtles and fish" (quoted in Sauer 1966).

Las Casas also provided an account of the natives of Cuba. In his 1516 memorandum to Cardinal Francisco Jiménez de Cisneros, he described four native groups who needed to be salvaged: those of the Jardines of both north and south Cuba; the Guanahacabibes of the Cape of Cuba; the Ciboneys, who were the same as those of the Jardines, but were kept as servants by the other Cuban Indians; and any left on the Lucayan islands who are described as of the same nature and ways as those of the Jardines (Lovén 1935; Keegan 1992). Clearly Las Casas had two classificatory groups in mind: the Guanahatabeys (i.e., the Guanahacabibes) and the people who have come to be called the Taínos (i.e., the Ciboneys, the Lucayans, and the people of the Jardines) (Keegan 1992).

But, although both Las Casas and Velázquez lived in Cuba for some time, they never visited western Cuba and thus lacked firsthand knowledge of the Guanahatabeys (Lovén 1935). When Pánfilo de Narváez entered the province of Habana he found caciques and conditions that were similar to those

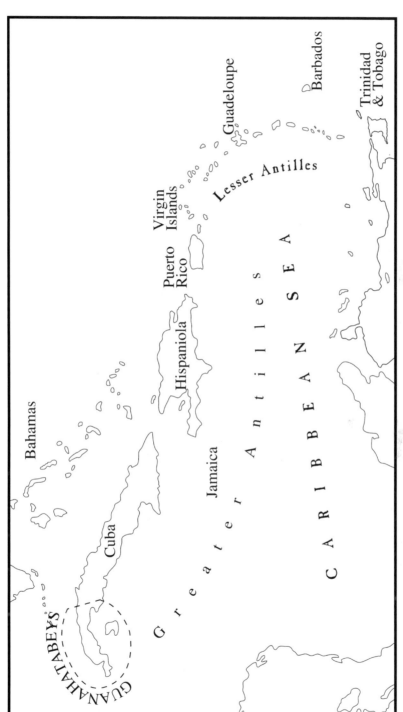

Figure 6.1. Guanahatabeys in western Cuba. (Adapted from Rouse, *The Taínos*. Used by permission.)

of eastern Cuba (Lovén 1935). In addition, five provinces of "chieftainships" have been identified in western Cuba from the reports of Diego Velázquez and Pánfilo de Narváez. These provinces bear the Taíno names (from west to east) Guanahacabibes, Guaniguanico, Marien, Habana, and Hanabana (Rouse 1948; Keegan 1992). Las Casas's and Velázquez's reports of hunters and fishers who lacked houses and agricultural fields and who lived in caves were apparently unsupported by firsthand observations of other Spanish officials.

Archaeological Investigations

The fact that the Guanahatabeys allegedly spoke a different language also indicates that they formed a separate ethnic group (Rouse 1992). Archaeological research has not identified any Taíno sites in western Cuba. What has been unearthed is the presence of a preexisting nonagricultural culture based on mostly uniformly small coastal sites. These sites contain a scatter of debris from tools, shellfish, iguanas, land and sea crabs, larger sea animals like manatee and turtles, and rodents such as the hutia (Rouse 1948). The evidence suggests the presence of people who lived in the open as well as in caves and relied heavily on shellfish, fish and game, and who were organized into small bands rather than villages. However, it has been argued that the archaeological data may in fact relate to native people ancestral to the Guanahatabeys (Rouse 1948). There may be no inherent contradiction between Pánfilo de Narváez's observations of a socially complex society comprising caciques (chiefs) in the western province of Habana and archaeological data found in western Cuba. The Calusa, also called the Shell People, lived in southwest Florida from 1500 to 1800, and despite their nonagricultural lifeways had a very socially complex society based on chiefdoms. It has been suggested that the Guanahatabeys may have been culturally affiliated with natives of southern Florida as their archaeological remains show some resemblances, especially in the shellwork and woodwork (Rouse 1992). To what extent these resemblances are the result of interaction or parallel adaptation to similar ecological conditions remains to be determined (Rouse 1992).

DNA

DNA techniques applied to forty-seven pre-Columbian skeletal samples purportedly belonging to the Guanahatabeys (Lalueza-Fox et al. 2003) point to South America and possibly Central America as their areas of origin. It is believed that the colonization of the Caribbean mainly took place in successive migration movements that emanated from the same area in South America, around the Lower Orinoco Valley: The first wave consisted of hunter-gatherer groups (ancestors of the Guanahatabeys) followed by a subsequent wave by agriculturalists (ancestors of Taínos in Puerto Rico) (Lalueza-Fox et al. 2003). Casimiroids migrated from Central America to Cuba and Hispaniola around 4000 B.C., so it is quite possible that the archaeological remains found in western Cuba may also be related to this Archaic population.

Conclusion

Even if Guanahatabeys is the accurate name for the inhabitants of western Cuba at contact, there are still many gray areas concerning this native group, assuming of course, that such a group actually existed. It is unclear whether the Guanahatabeys were a figment of Spanish or Taíno imagination or whether the archaeological materials found in western Cuba were generated by native forebears of the Guanahatabeys who inhabited western Cuba long before Spanish contact. It is also unclear whether the Guanahatabeys were culturally affiliated to the socially complex Calusa hunter-gatherers of southwestern Florida or to the pottery-making Casimiroids in Cuba. More intensive archaeology research should shed more light on issues of cultural affiliations and social complexity. What seems certain is that the Taínos did not occupy western Cuba at the time of contact, despite other evidence that the region was inhabited (Persons 2007). The debate concerning exactly who inhabited western Cuba during Spanish contact may not be resolved any time soon, given the controversial nature of Spanish ethnohistorical records on the subject. However, while the presence of Guanahatabeys in western Cuba may be a myth, to believe that Ciboneys lived in that same geographical space at Spanish contact is an even greater myth. The term Ciboney has been misapplied in the vast majority of history books.

Myth 7

The Island-Caribs
Were Cannibals

At the time of European contact there were people living in the Lesser
Antilles who resisted European invasion. Today we call them Island-
Caribs to differentiate them from the Caribs of South America. The
Island-Caribs of the Windward Islands are also referred to as Kalinagos
or Kalinas. Island-Carib ancestors have been depicted as cannibals and
therefore as the great villains of Caribbean history. But no evidence supports this conclusion.

◦

One of the greatest falsehoods still inscribed in our history books is the notion that the Island-Caribs were cannibals (Figure 7.1). The noble, peaceful
Greater Antillean Arawak versus the barbaric, savage Lesser Antillean Carib
was formalized as early as 1948 in the *Handbook of South American Indians*.
In the first chapter of James Michener's blockbuster historical novel *Caribbean,* the Island-Caribs are depicted as fierce, terrible cannibals who fought
unrelentingly against the Arawaks, not only to subdue them but also to eat
them. Equally negative portrayals of Island-Caribs are evident in more scholarly writings. One prominent scholar, for example, contended that the Island-
Carib men of the sixteenth and seventeenth centuries practiced ritualistic cannibalism. They "ate bits of the flesh of opposing warriors in order to acquire
the latter's prowess" (Rouse 1992). Depictions of Island-Carib cannibalism in
the 2006 movie *Pirates of the Caribbean: Dead Man's Chest,* which were vehe-
mently denounced in 2005 by the chief of Dominica's Carib (Kalinago) Indians, underscore the extent to which these ideas permeate the popular culture
of the day. No evidence, either archaeological or from firsthand observations
by Europeans, conclusively proves that Island-Caribs ever consumed human
flesh.

Human cannibalism is not unheard of. Recent history suggests that on oc-
casion "civilized" people have resorted to cannibalism in order to survive. The

Figure 7.1. Cannibal Indians, from a 1621 engraving, Venice.

story of the Donner Party is a tragic incident in American frontier history. A group of about ninety immigrants led by George Donner was caught in a blinding snowstorm high in the Sierra Nevada range of California in 1846. They made their way out in early 1847. They had resorted to eating the flesh of their dead comrades to survive. On October 13, 1972, Uruguayan Air Force Flight 571, carrying forty-five people, crashed in the Andes. Shortly after the rescue operation on December 23, 1972, it soon became evident that cannibalism had been widely practiced by the survivors. Cannibalism is also associated with sick and twisted minds such as the bizarre case of Germany's Armin Meiwes, who, in 2004, was tried and convicted for killing and eating someone he met through the Internet.

Defining Cannibalism

The first step in meeting the challenge of recognizing cannibalism in the archaeological is to define cannibalism. According to Myers (1984:149) there is an absence of a clear definition of cannibalism, a practice encompassing an extremely broad and sometimes ambiguous range of behaviors. Cannibalism can include drinking the diluted ashes of a cremated relative, licking blood off a sword in warfare (Sagan 1974:56), masticating and subsequently vomiting a snippet of human flesh (Tuzin and Brown 1983), or celebrating Christian communion. In this book, cannibalism is defined as humans consuming human tissue, whether this is done within the context of warfare, as part of a funeral rite, or for gastronomic or survival purposes. Three major classifications of cannibalism have been cited. Endocannibalism refers to consumption of individuals within the group; exocannibalism indicates consumption of outsiders; and autocannibalism covers everything from nail-biting to torture-induced self-consumption (Arens 1979).

Archaeological Perspectives on Cannibalism

The four lines of evidence important in verifying cannibalism in the archaeological record are

1. Similar butchering techniques in human and animal remains. Thus frequency, location, and type of verified cut marks and chop marks on human and animal bones must be similar, but we should allow for anatomical differences between humans and animals;
2. Similar patterns of long bone breakage that might facilitate marrow extraction
3. Identical patterns of postprocessing discard of human and animal remains
4. Evidence of cooking; if present, such evidence should indicate comparable treatment of human and animal remains. (Villa et al. 1986:431)

Even though identifying cannibalism in the archaeological record is sometimes problematic (as a host of postdepositional factors, unrelated to anthropophagy, can alter human bones in some archaeological contexts), a handful of sites with evidence of human cannibalism have been found outside the Caribbean. Examples include the 780,000-year-old hominid site of Gran Dolina in Sierra de Atapuerca, Spain (Fernandez-Jalvo et al. 1999) and the Navatu midden in Fiji, whose chronology spanned from 50 B.C. to A.D. 1900 (Degusta 1999). In addition, ritual cannibalism may have motivated the mortuary practices of the Middle pre-Ceramic period (ca. 6500–2000 B.C.) for the Nanchoc region of the upper Zaña Valley, northern Peru where careful breaking, cutting, and placement of human bones from adult males during the Las Pircas phase (6500–4000 B.C.) gave way to more haphazard breakage and discard during the subsequent Tierra Blanca phase (6000–3000 B.C.) (Rossen and Dillehay 2001).

The study of Mancos in southwestern Colorado in the United States is perhaps the most important research that conclusively points to cannibalism in pre-Columbian America (White 1992) (Figure 7.2). Based on a reexamination of more than two thousand fragmented, burnt, cut, and completely disarticulated human bones from an Anasazi pueblo, it was concluded that nearly thirty men, women, and children had been butchered and cooked there around A.D. 1100. Their bones were fractured for marrow and the remains discarded in several rooms of the pueblo. By comparing the human skeletal remains with those of animals used for food at other sites, the study revealed evidence of skinning, dismembering, cooking, and fracturing, leading to the inference that cannibalism took place at Mancos (White 1992) (Figure 7.3). Also identified was a new perimortem damage feature termed "pot polish" (Figure 7.4). It was shown, quite convincingly by experiment, and by Mancos Canyon statistics, that the projecting tips and spurs of some bone fragments are polished because they had likely been stirred around in rough pottery vessels.

To date, no such physical anthropological research has been conducted at Island-Carib sites in the Caribbean. The very fact that the Island-Caribs have largely been archaeologically invisible has no doubt complicated the issue (Keegan 1996a). Proper site identification is absolutely necessary before any useful physical anthropological research can be conducted in the field. To date, there are no confirmed Island-Carib sites, although contact-period sites in Grenada and St. Kitts that may relate to the Island-Caribs have been investigated (Cody 1995).

Previously, the Island-Caribs in the Caribbean were associated with a relatively crude style of pottery called Suazey after the Savanne Suazey site in Grenada where it was first identified (Bullen 1964). It has since been demonstrated that the people who manufactured Suazoid series pottery probably were not the historic Island-Caribs (Allaire 1984, 1991). Although contact sites on Grenada and St. Kitts have been investigated (Cody 1995; Farr 1995), it is unclear whether these are in fact Island-Carib. Moreover, the sites are few in number

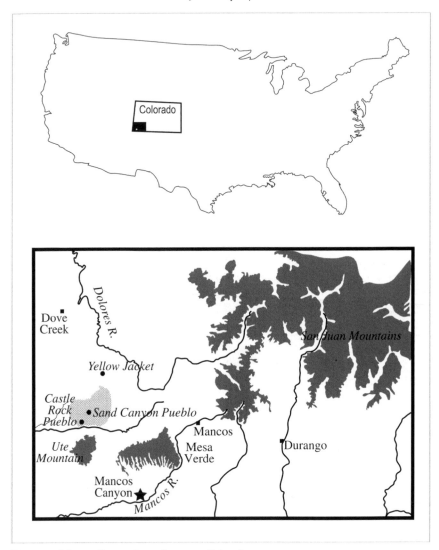

Figure 7.2. Mancos Canyon in southwestern Colorado.

and are difficult to positively identify on the ground. Given this level of uncertainty, it would be difficult for any physical anthropologist to successfully find butchered, charred, or pot polished human bones that incontrovertibly relate to these people.

The Mancos example has been cited as an excellent case of survival cannibalism (White 1992). But even if we accept the survival cannibalism hypothesis for Mancos, it is simply not logical to apply this to the Island-Caribs,

Figure 7.3. Burial remains from Mancos Canyon. (Used by permission of the Crow Canyon Archaeological Center.)

given the latter's expertise as hunters and fishers in such a protein-rich environment as the Caribbean. Indeed, the Lesser Antilles possessed productive resources in the form of rich offshore habitats (Wilson 2007) to which the Island-Caribs had easy access. In fact, some of the shallow shelves and banks surrounding islands—populated by a diverse collection of aquatic foods—are much larger than the islands themselves (Wilson 2007). Moreover, human beings, from time immemorial, have been able to successfully colonize environmentally unfriendly areas in the world (Fagan 2002) without resorting to cannibalism.

Problems with Ethnohistory

Clearly, claims of Island-Carib cannibalism are not based on archaeological evidence but rather on ethnohistory, that is, European accounts of native populations in the Caribbean. Ethnohistorical sources cannot be entirely trusted as they are often laden with racial and cultural biases (Hulme 1993). A critical reading of Columbus's *diario*—the so-called daily log of Columbus's first

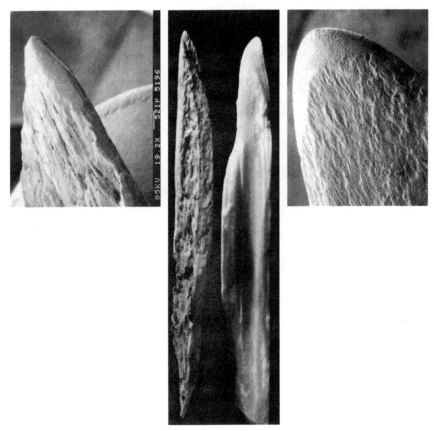

Figure 7.4. Human bones from Mancos Canyon showing evidence of pot polish and beveling.

voyage—reveals a litany of half-truths, anecdotal descriptions, hearsay, and preconceived Eurocentric ideas about the native peoples of the Caribbean (see Chapter 10). The November 4 entry in Columbus's diary has been interpreted as proof of the Admiral's knowledge of supposedly cannibalistic Carib Indians: "He [Columbus] understood also that, far from there, there were one-eyed men, and others, with snouts of dogs, who ate men, and that as soon as one was taken they cut his throat and drank his blood." Although Columbus's *diario* has influenced in some way all discussions of the peoples of the Lesser Antilles, the Admiral's first voyage never actually reached the Lesser Antilles (Keegan 1996b). A critical analysis of this document reveals a confusion of the following categories (Keegan 1996b):

1. *Cannibals:* Natives who refused to submit to the Spanish were called cannibals. They were characterized as idolaters and consumers of human flesh

who could not be converted into Christianity and were therefore suitable for enslaving.

2. *Caribes:* The Spanish understood Caribes to be real people when in fact they were creatures who existed only in Taíno mythology.

3. *Caniba:* Columbus sought an audience with the Grand Khan of Cathay (China). Caniba is the name Columbus gave to denote the Grand Khan's subjects.

In relation to item 1, there was simply no merit to those allegations as the so-called cannibals are essentially a legacy of the Spanish (Keegan 1992; Sued-Badillo 1978; Myers 1984). For several decades, history writers have created a false dichotomy of the "peaceful Arawaks" and the "man-eating cannibals." In light of the regular skirmishes between the Taínos and the Spaniards (which culminated with the battle of the Vega Real in 1495 [Figure 7.5]) (Wilson 1990), the notion of "peaceful Arawaks" was considerably overplayed. Despite native resistance, the Spanish were able to easily subjugate the Taínos in the northern Caribbean because the Taínos often attempted compromise and accommodation rather than warfare (Keegan 1992). The more militant Island-Caribs of the Lesser Antilles, who adopted more aggressive postures toward the Spanish, French, English, Dutch, and anyone else who threatened their sovereignty, were categorized as cannibals (Keegan 1992). In fact, the word *Carib* soon became a general Spanish term for hostile natives. For example, between 1815 and 1820, an area on the coast of northeastern Luzon, Philippines, was labeled Negroes Caribes Bravos (González 1988). The Island-Carib's aggressive responses to the European proved to be the more successful since they survived unconquered into the eighteenth century and beyond. Charles Williams, the chief of Dominica's Caribs, was accurate when he said that "our ancestors stood up against early European conquerors and because they stood up . . . we were labelled savages and cannibals up to today" (Reid 2005b).

The Island-Caribs tenaciously fought European attempts to colonize their islands for nearly two centuries. Today, their descendants live in various eastern and southern Caribbean territories, principally Dominica, St. Vincent, and Trinidad (Wilson 2007; Allaire 1997; Gonzalez 1988; Reid 2005c). But another reason for this survival revolved around the fact that the Europeans were not particularly interested in the Lesser Antilles for the first two centuries after contact, although many of these small islands were depopulated by continuous raids by the Spaniards in search of Indian labor for the Greater Antilles. Despite this, the Spaniards were far more interested in the Greater Antilles and subsequently in Mexico and Peru; these territories held the greater promise of gold to fill the Spanish Crown's coffers (Birmingham 2000). In addition, when compared to the Taínos of the northern Caribbean, the Island-Caribs survived

El Almᵗᵉ. descubre las yslas delos Lucayos que fueron las primeras de Indias.

Figure 7.5. The Battle of the Vega Real, Hispaniola, April 1495.

the influx of European diseases more successfully (Hulme 1986; Wilson 1997). They typically lived in smaller villages and were more mobile (Wilson 2007). Although they suffered from disease and raids, they could take their canoes and flee from Europeans who might attack or attempt to enslave them. There is also evidence that continuous migration by the Island-Caribs from South America may have helped maintain some Indian presence in the Lesser Antilles (Keegan 2000; L. Antonio Curet, personal communication 2007).

The Spanish distinction between "peaceful" Taínos and "warlike" Caribs was not without self-interest. At the outset, Columbus seemed to have in mind the development of a slave trade similar to the Portuguese operation in Africa (Keegan 1992). Those people whom Columbus believed could be transformed into holiness through conversion to Christianity came to be known by history writers as the "peaceful Arawaks" (Black 1983; Dookhan 2006), while those who resisted were pagans who deserved to be enslaved. In fact, agitation against slave taking by priests who managed Spain's missionary efforts in the Greater Antilles caused the Crown to forbid slave taking among Indians who were friendly to the Spanish (Keegan 1992). But in response to economic interests, Queen Isabel in 1503 excluded from this ban "all cannibals." These "cannibals" were legally defined as barbaric people, enemies of the Christian, those who refuse conversion, and those who eat human flesh (Sauer 1966).

These Eurocentric categories were extended to much of the Caribbean, including Trinidad. It was, therefore, difficult to ascertain how many Carib Indians were present in Trinidad at the time of Columbus's arrival in 1498, as the Spanish, in their anxiety to enslave the Indians, were quick to designate areas of the Caribbean's most southerly island as Carib (Newson 1976). For example, in 1510, it was said that there were no peaceful Indians along the whole coast of Tierre Firme, except in Trinidad, but in 1511 the latter was declared Carib. In 1532, Governor Sedeño petitioned the Crown for permission to enslave the Indians of Trinidad on the grounds that they were "Caribs and people who eat human flesh and have other rites and evil customs and are very warlike" (Newson 1976).

Preoccupation with Cannibalism

At the heart of the matter was the European preoccupation with cannibalism (Arens 1979). Several anthropologists (primarily of European decent) have displayed an obsession with cannibalism, leading one writer to argue: " In the deft hands and fertile imaginations of anthropologists, former or contemporary anthropophagists have multiplied with the advance of civilization and fieldwork in formerly unstudied culture areas. The existence of man-eating peoples just beyond the pale of civilization is a common ethnographic suggestion" (Arens 1979).

Perhaps one of the most obvious examples of this can be found in the oft-reprinted tract of Amerigo Vespucci (after whom the continents of the New World were named) (Berkhofer 1979). Vespucci's early sixteenth-century tract was important in establishing the early conception and imagery of the Indian. The following is an extract from the Florentine's alleged experiences with the natives of Brazil (Berkhofer 1979): "I knew a man whom I also spoke to who was reputed to have eaten more than three hundred bodies. And I likewise remained twenty-seven days in a certain city where I saw salted flesh suspended from beams between the houses, just as with us it is the custom to hang bacon and pork." This bizarre and incredible account of Vespucci in his *Mundus Novus* (published around 1504–5) reinforced the ambiguous images of the New World Indians in the minds of educated Europeans, for its publication was even more widespread than Columbus's diary and its description of Indian customs was far more detailed and vivid (Berkhofer 1979).

The dichotomies of heavenly tropical paradise versus an unfriendly hellish jungle, of good, noble savages versus vicious, evil cannibals have for centuries been an intrinsic part of the Europeans' attitude toward the New World. For example, Columbus described the Taínos of the northern Caribbean as peaceful, docile natives in his widely published letter of 1493 (Berkhofer 1979). In contrast to this favorable view of Taínos, the Admiral provided the first negative image of the New World: "In these islands I have found so far no human monstrosities, as many expected, but on the contrary the whole population is very well formed. . . . Thus I have found no monsters, nor had a report of any, except in an island 'Carib,' which is the second at the coming into the Indies, which is inhabited by a people who are regarded in all the islands as very fierce and who eat human flesh." This mind-set, which classified non-Western, preliterate societies as either noble savages or cannibals, was often imputed by Europeans to people beyond their cultural horizon. It was a brazen attempt to dehumanize non-Westerners, therefore justifying their brutal subjugation. "This form of othering" (de Albuquerque 1974) (seeing Europeans as distinct from subordinate groups lumped together as "the other") is part of Western ideology of colonialism, missionization, and cultural imperialism.

But the preoccupation with cannibalism was not restricted to European explorers; it was deeply entrenched in Taíno mythology (Keegan 1996b). Columbus's *diario* refers to Taíno accounts of flesh-eating Caribes. They removed people from their villages, who never returned, and they consumed human flesh. This, however, has been interpreted as reference to "the prohibition against return migration rather than to anthropophagy" (Stevens-Arroyo 1988). Interestingly, there is a mythical association between the Spanish colonizers and Caribes in a prophecy recorded by Fray Ramón Pané, the Jeronymite friar commissioned by Columbus to record the Taíno religion (Keegan 1996b). In short, the Taínos identified Columbus and his crew as Caribes, or cannibals. If cannibals had truly been known to the Taínos, they would not have confused them with these early Europeans.

Conclusion

The issue of Island-Carib cannibalism owes its persistence to inaccurate interpretations of linguistic and ethnohistorical data and the lack of archaeological evidence supporting such claims. Although these allegations have no basis in fact, our history books continue to churn out literary fantasies about Island-Carib cannibalism. Movies like *Pirates of the Caribbean: Dead Man's Chest* are also active agents of this type of propaganda peddling. Here in the Caribbean, the need for historical accuracy is both relevant and immediate, given the presence of the Santa Rosa Carib community in Arima, Trinidad, and Island-Carib descendants in both Dominica and St. Vincent. Inasmuch as the myth of Island-Carib cannibalism has become a part of popular thinking, by disseminating historically accurate information (particularly to our young people), we can eventually disabuse people's minds of this myth.

All the Amerindians Migrating from South America to the Caribbean Island-Hopped from the Continent to the Lesser and Greater Antilles

It is generally assumed that all the Amerindians who migrated from South America into the Caribbean island-hopped from the continent, taking advantage of favorable trade winds and ocean currents. However, archaeological evidence and computer simulations suggest that while a majority of native groups island-hopped from South America, some may have jumped directly from South America to the northern Lesser Antilles and Puerto Rico.

∾

Island-Hopping

For years, it was generally assumed that all the precolonial peoples from South America who had migrated into the Caribbean, island-hopped from the Lesser Antilles to the Greater Antilles. However, archaeological evidence also points to the likelihood of "direct jumps" by Saladoid migrants from South America to the northern Caribbean. It is easy to understand why these early precolonials were engaged in island-hopping. Most of the islands in the Lesser Antilles are within sight of each other, which would have facilitated travel (Rouse 1992). For instance, Trinidad and Grenada are joined by intersecting visibility ranges, thus posing a scenario in which both landmasses are actually within sight of each other (Figure 8.1). When at sea, before navigators lose visual contact with their place of origin, they are able to detect the presence of another landmass (e.g., traveling from the Orinoco to Trinidad). These critical spaces of intersecting visibility provided a continuum between islands (Torres and Reniel Rodríguez 2008). Computer simulations suggest that canoes paddled in shifts could have reached the closest islands to South America in several days with little risk of death (Callaghan 2001). In such a situation, the precolonial mari-

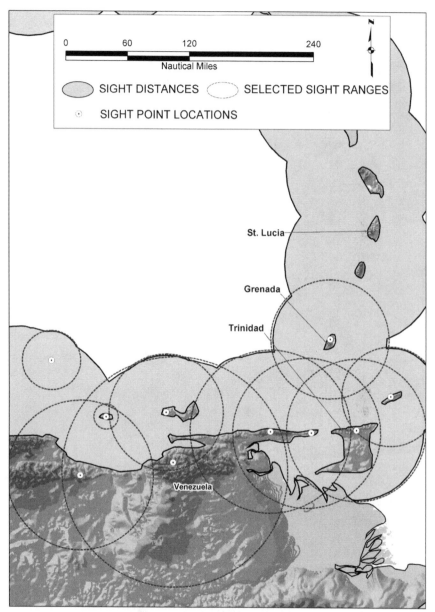

Figure 8.1. Overlapping visibility areas in the Lesser Antilles. *Note:* Areas of visibility overlap where multiple islands are visible from one another.

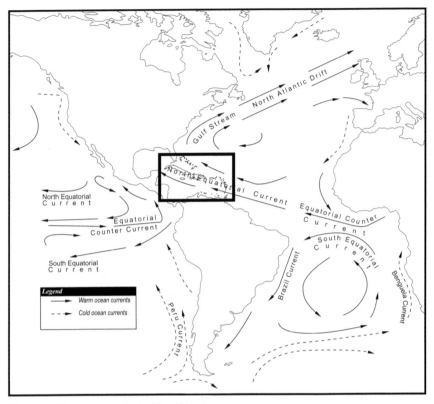

Figure 8.2. Ocean currents in the New World.

ners could have navigated throughout the Caribbean using heavy cloud cover to indicate where islands existed.

Furthermore, the currents and trade winds in the Caribbean favor travel from south to north and from east to west (Figures 8.2 and 8.3). The North Equatorial Current originates from the northwestern coast of Africa, where it is fed mainly by the cooler waters flowing from the northeast Atlantic. As the North Equatorial Current travels across the open ocean, it is joined by waters originating south of the equator, thus trapping waters from the Southern Atlantic into the Northern Atlantic (Bischof et al. 2004). The North Equatorial Current is deflected northward along the coast of the Guianas. The Orinoco River, with its massive outpouring of fresh water at its mouth, also helps to divert part of this powerful current northward. The remainder of the current continues in a westerly direction along the coast of South America and northward past Central America into the Gulf of Mexico and the Florida straits eventually becoming the Gulf Stream. Trade winds, which blow steadily from

Figure 8.3, Trade winds and currents in the Caribbean.

the northeast during most of the year, reinforce the westward-moving currents (Rouse 1992). The general assumption was that precolonial peoples, by taking advantage of favorable current and wind conditions, island-hopped from the southernmost islands of the Caribbean to the northern Caribbean.

Saladoid Migration

However, while the majority of native groups island-hopped from South America into the Caribbean, archaeological evidence also points to the likelihood of direct jumps from South America to the northern Caribbean. Until recently, it was generally assumed that the dispersal of Saladoid peoples into the West Indies only involved island-by-island northward expansion of a single Saladoid culture (Keegan 2000). Recent investigations indicate instead that there was a direct jump from Venezuela to the Leeward Islands, U.S. Virgin Islands (St. Thomas, St. Croix, and St. John), and eastern Puerto Rico (Callaghan 1995). Radiocarbon dates from the Hope estate site on St. Martin and the Trants and Radio Antilles sites on Montserrat indicate that they were settled around 500 B.C. (Hofman and Hoogland 1999; Petersen 1996) around the time when the Saladoids started to migrate into the Caribbean. It has also been noted that the earliest Ceramic-age sites (500 B.C. to A.D. 1) are located in Puerto Rico, the U.S. Virgin Islands, and the Leeward Islands (Haviser 1997). Movement was so rapid that arrival in eastern Puerto Rico was almost simultaneous with departure from Trinidad/South America. By calculating the reproductive potential of these indigenes, it is clear that they could not have reproduced fast enough to sequentially settle the islands in such a short space of time (Keegan 1995). Therefore in all probability there were direct jumps from the South American mainland to the northern Lesser Antilles and Puerto Rico (Figure 8.4).

Carib Watercraft Design

For years, it was assumed that precolonial natives in South America, given their apparent lack of ships and sails, resorted to traveling up and down the chain of islands, rather than across the Caribbean Sea (Rouse 1992). But the discovery of the Carib skeg design in the Upper Orinoco region of Venezuela has opened up the possibility that natives in South America may have been capable of navigating across the Caribbean Sea using indigenous watercraft (Callaghan 2007). The small skeg or fin was attached toward the stern of small canoes (Figures 8.5 and 8.6). Informants in the Upper Orinoco region have indicated that this element was of considerable antiquity and was therefore unlikely to have been of European introduction. The skeg, which functions to

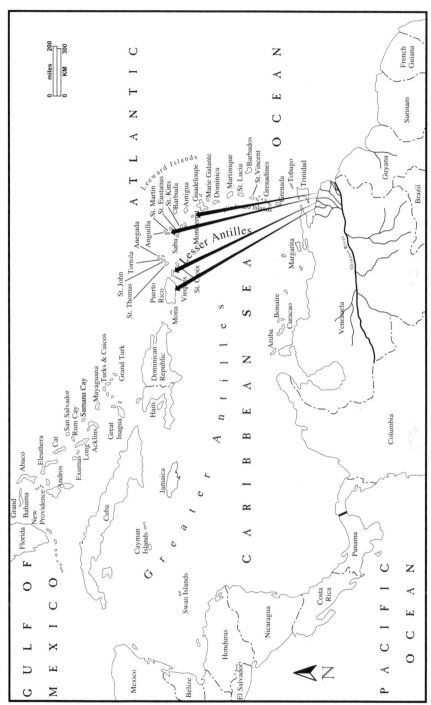

Figure 8.4. Direct jumps by Saladoid groups from South America to the northern Lesser Antilles and Puerto Rico.

Figure 8.5. Traditional Greenland kayak skeg used by the Inuits. (From Callaghan, "Survival of a Traditional Carib Watercraft Design Element." Photograph by Matt Walls. Used by permission.)

orient the canoe in rough waters and rapids, may have been used by precolonial navigators across the Caribbean Sea. A similar element is found in the design of some traditionally based watercraft in Martinique and may represent part of a much wider distribution (Callaghan 2007). However, boat technology is not the only factor required for traveling long distances across the Caribbean Sea. Knowledge about the prevailing winds and currents, weather patterns, steering and maintaining a course, the use of celestial features for guidance, location of islands before they are visible (Curet 2005), and wayfinding based on heavy cloud cover over islands are needed as well.

Directly traversing the Caribbean Sea from South America and landing in the northern Caribbean would not have posed an insurmountable challenge for the indigenes. The Caribbean is an open saltwater sea, with an approximate area of 2.75 million km² (1.04 million mi²), a length of 2,414 km (1,500 mi), and a width of about 563 km (350 mi). Crossing such a relatively small body of water would not have been an insurmountable challenge for early Saladoid migrants from northeast South America. After 2000 B.C., the early Polynesians successfully crossed the Pacific Ocean, where islands are sometimes thou-

Figure 8.6. Carib skeg. (From Callaghan, "Survival of a Traditional Carib Watercraft Design Element." Used by permission.)

sands of kilometers from one another. The successful settlement of Polynesia and Melanesia was closely connected to the cultivation of yams and taro (Fagan 2005). This enabled people to live on islands far from the mainland landmasses, too isolated for animals or plants to migrate to. Such voyages by the early navigators of the Pacific took place in oceangoing hulled canoes capable of carrying heavy loads (Fagan 2005). In short, we should not underestimate the ability of precolonial peoples to explore vast expanses of water, whether the Pacific, the Atlantic, or the Caribbean. With appropriate technology and knowledge, ancients were able to travel extremely long distances with a high probability of survival (Irwin 1992; Curet 2005).

Computer Simulations

Computer simulations by Richard Callaghan also support direct jumps from South America to the northern Caribbean. By using two types of seafaring vessels, the platform and stargaze canoes, in a computer program that tracks a vessel's movement due to unintentional drifting or paddling, Callaghan's experiments indicate that although direct jumps from South America to the northern Antilles were possible, they were more accidental than deliberate (Callaghan 2001). Chance discoveries, through drifting, would have been unlikely and dangerous. Nevertheless, the study concludes that chance discoveries could have occurred (Callaghan 2001). These chance discoveries would have led the Saladoids to discover the northern Antilles before the southernmost islands, which goes against commonsense explanations (Callaghan 2001).

However, not all the landings in the northern Antilles may have been the result of chance discoveries. Line of sight analyses with the aid of geographical information systems technology have demonstrated that precolonial interaction and travel throughout the region may have been facilitated by landscape intervisibility, including the possibility of direct travel from South America to the Greater Antilles (Torres and Reniel Rodríguez 2008) (Figure 8.7). As humans interacted with their visual surroundings at sea, they most likely developed connections of spatial relationality that were used to orient themselves within the Caribbean during sea travel (Torres and Reniel Rodríguez 2008; Ingold 2000; Irwin 1992). The relatively long distance between South America and Greater Antilles has been used as an argument against the possibility of direct contacts between them. However, if one takes into consideration the extended visual ranges observed in northeastern Colombia and southern Hispaniola, then the distance for making a virtual landfall decreases from 463 to 236 nautical miles, which is just 115 nautical miles longer than the negative space of the Anegada Passage (Torres and Reniel Rodríguez 2008) separating the British Virgin Islands and Anguilla. This dramatically increases the chances of accidentally detecting the Greater Antilles and provides further support for the modeling of navigational routes to the Caribbean from South America, as proposed by Callaghan (2003) (Torres and Reniel Rodríguez 2008).

Migrations from Central America

The presence of Casimiroid sites in Cuba and Hispaniola supports the idea that several migrants apparently voyaged from the Yucatán peninsula. A countercurrent moves eastward along the southern side of the Greater Antilles and this would have facilitated travel from Yucatán to the Greater Antilles (Rouse 1992). Using winds, currents, and other conditions of the natural environment as variables, Callaghan's computer simulations clearly indicate that while the route from the Yucatán to Cuba was possible, it was far easier migrating from South America (Callaghan 1990).

Conclusion

The evidence presented points to the adaptability and resilience of early native migrants to the Caribbean. Radiocarbon dates have confirmed that there were direct jumps from the mainland to the northern Lesser Antilles and Puerto

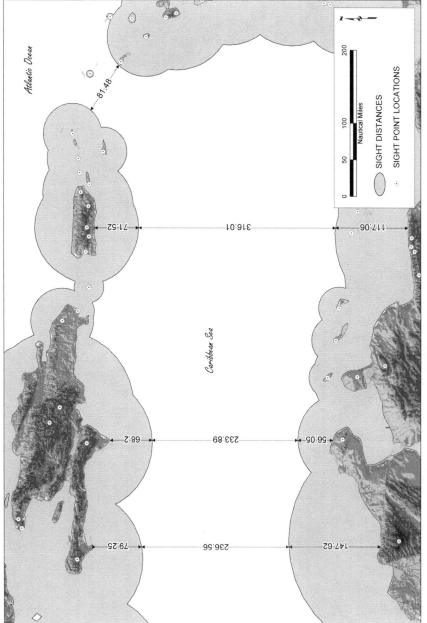

Figure 8.7. Variability in distances between coasts and landmass visibility ranges.

Rico. Even if some of these direct jumps were accidental, the ability of pre-colonial peoples to adapt and to travel by sea over relatively long distances (using their knowledge of sea currents and trade winds) speaks volumes about their innate abilities as boat-builders and mariners. Such capabilities also made early migration from Central America to the Greater Antilles possible.

Myth 9

The Spanish Introduced Syphilis into the Caribbean and the New World

Spanish colonizers have been justifiably vilified for their atrocities against the Taínos and for introducing a host of diseases to the New World. However, one disease that was already present in the New World prior to European contact was syphilis.

∽

It is generally accepted that by far the most prevalent cause of Amerindian mortality in the New World were European-introduced diseases such as smallpox, scarlet fever, measles, influenza, typhoid fever, cholera, yellow fever, dengue fever, and amoebic dysentery (Crosby 1986; Bryan 1992). Syphilis, a contagious sexually transmitted disease caused by the spirochete *Treponema pallidum* (Figure 9.1), has been cited as yet another disease introduced to the New World by the Spanish colonizers (Desowitz 1997; McGregor 2007). This argument is based on the premise that syphilis was an old European disease that had been improperly diagnosed as leprosy prior to 1500 (Desowitz 1997; McGregor 2007). But was syphilis really introduced into the New World by the Spanish or was this virulent disease strain already present in the Americas before Christopher Columbus's arrival?

Ancient and Medieval Sources

Ancient and medieval sources have long been cited as evidence for syphilis in Europe before Columbus, but none of the descriptions by Greek and Roman authors was specific enough to be irrefutable. Returning crusaders brought "Saracen ointment" containing mercury for treating "lepers," an appropriate medication for syphilis but not for leprosy. Thirteenth- and fourteenth-century A.D. references to "venereal leprosy" may also indicate syphilis because leprosy is not sexually transmitted (Rose 1997). However, for several years, a number of

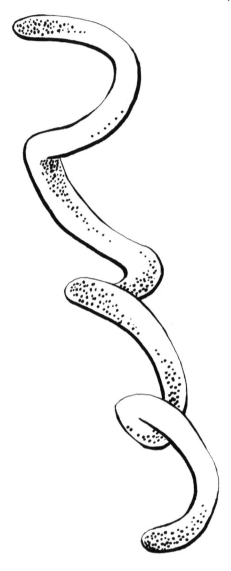

Figure 9.1. Image of spiral-shaped organism that causes syphilis.

archaeologists, historians, and paleopathologists have argued that syphilis was in fact in the Americas prior to the advent of the Spanish colonizers. Immediately after Columbus returned from his first voyage, a syphilis epidemic broke out in the Mediterranean, which suggests that syphilis was already present in the New World before then (Sauer 1966). Physicians, surgeons, and laymen of the Old World who wrote about syphilis in the sixteenth century recorded, with few exceptions, that it was a new malady (Figure 9.2) (Crosby 2003).

Figure 9.2. The preparation and use of guaiacum in the treatment of syphilis. From an engraving by Jan van der Straet. This illustration of a sickroom interior shows the stages in the preparation of an infusion for the treatment of the disease. (Impression in the Wellcome Library of the History of Medicine.)

Complexity of the Issues

But the issues relating to venereal syphilis in the New World are not as simple as they appear. Archaeologists and paleopathologists have examined thousands of skeletons from archaeological sites throughout North America, searching for definitive proof of pre-Columbian treponemal disease that would support the notion that the New World, not the Old, was the origin of this disease. Their endeavors have yielded a body of information that is both abundant and highly suggestive (Powell and Cook 2005). Since the 1940s, however, worldwide clinical and epidemiological studies of nonvenereal forms of treponemal disease that exist today alongside venereal syphilis have teased out several distinctions in key aspects of their epidemiology, pathology, immunology, and microbiology (Powell and Cook 2005). The bacterial pathogens associated with various diseases at first appeared to be identical to one another based on their morphological characteristics (Schell and Musher 1983), but recent techniques of microbial DNA analysis (Cameron et al. 1999; Centurion-Lara et al. 2000) have now seriously challenged the identification of all precolonial skeletons in the New World of treponemal origin as relating to venereal syphilis (Powell and Cook 2005). It is clear that treponemal disease has been present in various forms in the New World before European contact and these forms include at least four known subspecies of treponemal diseases: *T. palladium palladium,* which causes syphilis; *T. pallidum pertenue,* which causes yaws; *T. palladium carateum,* which causes pinta; and *T. palladium endemicum,* which causes bejel.

Moreover, the debate about the geographic origins of syphilis is far from over. Skeletal remains with evidence of the disease have come from medieval England (Hunnius et al. 2005), third- to fifth-century France and ancient Greek sites at Metaponto in Italy. A possible case from Iron Age southern Africa has also been cited (Steyn and Henneberg 1995). Despite this, the weight of the evidence strongly suggests a New World origin (Rose 1997; Rothschild et al. 2000, 2005). Research has allowed scientists to clearly separate syphilis from other diseases in its class of treponematoses (Rothschild 2005). Examination of skeletons from populations with clinically diagnosed bejel and yaws revealed bone alterations distinctive to those diseases, clearly separating them from alterations due to syphilis, transcending the limitations of current DNA and immunologic technologies. These insights have allowed us to confidently identify the New World as the origin of syphilis (Rothschild 2005). Furthermore, the absence of skeletal evidence of any treponemal disease in continental Europe before the time of Columbus excludes it as site of origin of syphilis. Treponemal disease appears to have originated in East Africa with late transmission to England, perhaps as a complication of the slave trade, with the original treponemal disease apparently spreading from Africa through Asia and then entering North America, where approximately eight thousand years later, it mutated to syphilis (Rothschild 2005).

Signs of Syphilis

If not treated, syphilis can cause serious effects, including damage to the heart, aorta, brain, eyes, and bones. In some cases these effects are fatal. In archaeological contexts, usual signs of syphilis are extensive destruction in the upper part of the skull in addition to marked striations and pitting of the long bones. However, as syphilis is a treponemal disease like yaws and rickets, it only leaves markings on the bones in its terminal phase (Figure 9.3) and is easily confused with similar markings made by other diseases. Paleopathological studies by Bruce and Christine Rothschild favor a New World origin (Rose 1997). After examining 687 skeletons from archaeological sites in the United States and Ecuador ranging from 400 to 6,000 years old, the Rothschilds discovered that the native populations to the south (New Mexico, Florida, and Ecuador)

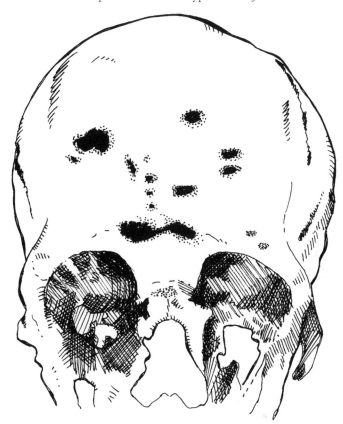

Figure 9.3. Syphilitic damage to the human skull.

had syphilis, while those to the north (Ohio, Illinois, and Virginia) had yaws. By contrast, examination of 1,000 Old World skeletons dated to before contact with the New World revealed no cases of syphilis. This suggests that syphilis was first present in the New World and was later brought to the Old World. Furthermore, the Rothschilds found that the earliest yaws cases in the New World collections were at least 6,000 years old, while the first syphilis cases were at least 800 years old and perhaps more than 1,600 years old. This suggests that syphilis may be a New World mutation of yaws, which has a world-wide distribution (Rose 1997). Clearly, the occurrence of the same mutation giving rise to syphilis independently in both the New and Old Worlds seems unlikely.

Olivier Dutour of the faculty of medicine at Marseilles, France, has concluded that the skeleton of a seven-month-old fetus at Costebelle, France, dated to fourth-century A.D., had lesions from congenital syphilis (Rose

1997). On the face of it, this example contributes to the argument that venereal syphilis did exist in the Old World before 1493 and that syphilis was
carried to the New World from the Old World by Columbus's crew. However, upon examining the Costebelle skeleton, Bruce Rothschild contended
that the Costebelle case was the result of lithopedion rather than congenital
syphilis. "Stone children," or lithopedion, a rarity occurring in only 0.0045 per-
cent of pregnancies, is caused by the calcification of a fetus or of fetal mem-
branes (Rose 1997). The condition was first described in a treatise on surgery
by Albucasis (A.D. 936–1013). The Rothschilds and Leland Bement (an archaeologist at the University of Texas, Austin) have identified a 3,100-year-old
lithopedion case at the Bering Sinkhole site in Texas (Rose 1997).

Tangible proof of precolonial syphilis in the Caribbean has been documented in the work of Bruce Rothschild and associates in the Dominican Republic (Rothschild et al. 2000). After examining 536 skeletons from the El
Soco, Juan Dolio, La Caleta, Atajadizo, and Cueva Cabrera sites in the Dominican Republic, which collectively date from 4,560 to 600 years ago, the authors concurred that syphilis was present in an area where Columbus actually
had contact years after. Therefore, the Admiral and his crew could easily have
contracted it from these native groups, subsequently spreading it from the New
World to the Old (Rothschild et al. 2000).

Conclusion

Syphilis, it seems, developed in the New World from yaws, perhaps 1,600 years
ago, and was waiting for Columbus and his crew when they arrived. The Taínos may have given the Spanish invaders syphilis (Rouse 1992) as their myths
describe its symptoms, and lesions on their skeletons could have been syphilis related. Another theory is that American syphilis hybridized with similar
treponemal diseases already in Europe such as yaws, and that this crossing produced a much more virulent strain of the disease (Crosby 2003; Rouse 1992).
The available evidence forces us to critically examine this aspect of our history
rather than blaming all of the maladies in the New World on Christopher Columbus and his crew.

Myth 10

Christopher Columbus Wrote the Version of His *Diario* (Diary) That We Use Today

During his first voyage to the Americas, Christopher Columbus kept a detailed daily journal in which he recorded sailing directions and distances, described the places he visited, and wrote about the native peoples he encountered. This journal has come to be known as the *diario de a bordo*. The original was presented to the king and queen of Spain at the end of the voyage but has since been lost. The question at hand is "who wrote the version of the *diario* that we use today?" Research has shown that Bartolomé de las Casas actually wrote most of it, based on third-hand transcriptions.

～

Columbus's *diario* contained the only eyewitness accounts of the Admiral's first voyage to the Caribbean (Dunn and Kelly 1989). These accounts supposedly described the territorial control of a powerful chief; the use of canoes and other products; trade; the personal adornments of the natives encountered; and environmental conditions that might be used to identify archaeological sites that were occupied at contact (Keegan 1996a). Christopher Columbus wrote a diary with details of his first voyage (Figure 10.1), with the original manuscript rendered by Diego Colon, son of Columbus. However, most of what we refer today as Columbus's diary, or *diario de a bordo,* was written by Bartolomé de las Casas. In October 1492, Christopher Columbus began writing his first impressions of Guanahani (San Salvador), the island in the Bahamas where he first made landfall in the New World. Columbus presented the original *diario* to Queen Isabella in 1493. She had a copy made for Columbus. But the whereabouts of the original are unknown, and all trace of the copy disappeared in 1545.

Thirdhand Manuscript

A thirdhand manuscript, written sometime in the mid-sixteenth century by Bartolomé de las Casas, survived, but it remained unpublished until the end of

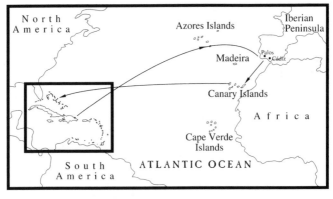

——————— Columbus' First Voyage (1492 -1493)

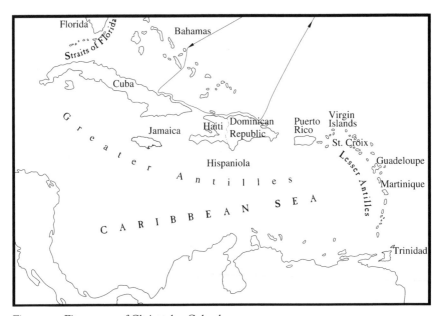

Figure 10.1. First voyage of Christopher Columbus, 1492–93.

the eighteenth century. With the exception of the one extensive first-person quotation ("the very words of the Admiral"), which covers Columbus's sojourn through the Bahamas (October 11–24, 1492), most of the *diario* consists of abstractions transcribed in the third person (Keegan 1996b). It is unclear what Las Casas was copying, except that it almost certainly was not the original text.

It has been argued that Columbus's *diario* bears comparatively little relationship to the text Columbus originally wrote, as this thirdhand manuscript has numerous erasures, unusual spellings, brief questionable passages, and notes in the margins. The ambiguities, errors, and omissions in this manuscript have been further compounded in modern-language translations (Keegan 1996b). Little is known about the circumstances under which Las Casas transcribed Columbus's text. It has also been argued that Las Casas transcribed the *diario* as an adjunct to compiling his massive *Historia de las Indias,* but given that this was almost a lifetime project, the transcription could have been made at any time throughout Las Casas's long writing career, though a date of 1552 has been suggested (Henige 1991).

Columbus's Diary and Archaeological Research

One of the most telling influences of Columbus's *diario* on archaeological research is the dichotomy of the peaceful Arawaks in the Greater Antilles and the Bahamas versus the Carib cannibals in the Lesser Antilles. The *diario* gives the impression that under no circumstances was contact possible between the northern and southern Caribbean territories. However, archaeological investigations have revealed that there were regular trade networks between the Greater Antilles, the Virgin Islands, and the northern Lesser Antilles, which gave rise to new cultural expressions (Hofman et al. 2007) (see Chapter 2). Although there are allegations of Island-Carib-cannibalism in Columbus's *diario,* no verifiable archaeological evidence has been found to substantiate such claims (see Chapter 7). The diary vividly describes the natives encountered by Columbus as simple people with a simple way of life, but archaeological research has revealed the presence of socially complex societies in the northern Caribbean at the time of Spanish contact (see Chapter 11).

Columbus's *diario* can be used in search of Columbus's landfall in the New World as it provides the only eyewitness accounts of the Lucayan Taínos in the Bahamas (Dunn and Kelly 1989). These accounts should enable archaeologists to identify Columbus's route, because the diary described the locations of seven Lucayan settlements on four separate islands. Lucayan sites are irregularly distributed such that only one route will have sites in the appropriate locations (Keegan 1996a). The comparison of precolonial settlement data along the various routes led William Keegan (1996a) to conclude that the first landfall must have been on present-day San Salvador, and that Columbus then proceeded to Rum Bay, Long Island, and Crooked Island before crossing to Cuba and then Hispaniola (Keegan 1996a) (Figure 10.2). Excavations at the Long Bay site on San Salvador Island (Hoffman 1987a, 1987b) have unearthed an assortment of European trade items, including green and yellow glass beads, a coin, brass D-rings, and a brass buckle. These materials are consistent with items known to have been carried on Columbus's ships (Brill et al. 1987; Hoffman 1987b).

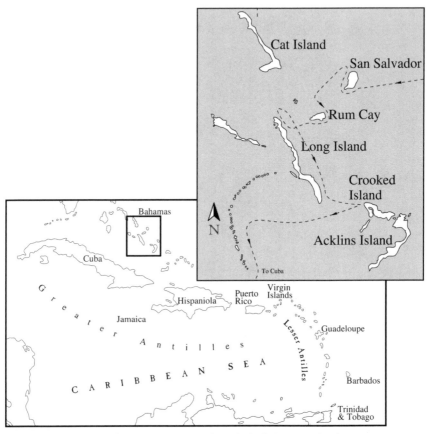

Figure 10.2. Christopher Columbus's journeys through the Bahamas on his first voyage.

Conclusion

The version of Columbus's *diario* that we use today was written by Bartolomé de las Casas, based on thirdhand transcriptions, and therefore should not be uncritically accepted and utilized. Like many other historical materials, the *diario* should be corroborated and tested against other data sources such as archaeology and ethnography to ensure greater levels of accuracy and consistency.

Myth 11

The Spanish Colonists Brought "Civilization" to Native Societies in the Caribbean

The word *civilization* has a variety of meanings. However, for the purposes of this chapter, it will be defined as "a society in an advanced state of social, economic, and political development." Contrary to popular Eurocentric thinking, Spanish colonists did not bring civilization to native societies in the Caribbean. When the Spanish arrived in the late fifteenth century, they found advanced systems already established on the islands in the northern Caribbean.

⁓

The word *civilization* comes from the Latin *civis,* meaning "citizen" or "townsman." It has been used in reference to a social process, as well as the quality of excellence in thought, manners, and taste. It is also considered to be a state-level society (Fagan 2002), which is the final stage of development from simple to more complex societies. However, for the purposes of this chapter, *civilization* is defined as "a society with an advanced state of social, economic, and political development."

The Noble Savage

Although Columbus did not clearly understand the culture of the islanders he encountered on his first voyage, in his widely published letter of 1493, he described with confidence the lifestyles of those people he called Indians: "The people of this island and all of the other islands which I found and of which I have information, all go about naked, men and women, as their mothers bore them. . . . They have no iron or steel or weapons, nor are they fitted to use them. . . . They are content with whatever trifle of whatever kind that may be given to them, whether it be of value or valueless" (Berkhofer 1979). The foregoing suggests simplicity, naïveté, and a lack of sophisticated technology. These stereotypes effectively framed European perceptions of societies outside of the western European center of Christianity, a perception in which non-Europeans were either noble savages or human monstrosities. The depiction of the noble savage resides in the doctrine of the goodness of humans as expounded in the first decade of the seventeenth century by Anthony Ashley Cooper, the Third Earl of Shaftesbury. Noble savage expresses notions of the goodness of humans, their simplicity of manners, and their innocent behavior, without the corrupting influence of civilization. The noble savage was the man of nature who lived according to the dictates of natural law, thought according to natural reason, and understood God and creation by way of natural religion. Columbus came to the New World with these Eurocentric attitudes in which he saw these precolonial peoples as childlike, innocent, without laws or institutions, and by extension incapable of self-government. In short, his thinking provided a convenient justification for European colonization.

Although still documented in some of our history books (Claypole and Robottom 2001; Black 1983), these negative stereotypes are simply not supported by archaeological and ethnohistorical data. Research has shown that the Taínos enjoyed an advanced level of social development (as evidenced by their stone-lined plazas, regional, district, and local chiefdoms); possessed sophisticated ceramic, stone, shell, and wood technologies; and had well-established trading relations with their Caribbean neighbors as well as with neighbors outside of the Caribbean.

Definition of Chiefdoms

The concept of the chiefdom was first formally advanced by Kalervo Oberg in 1955, and the core of it is simply that a chiefdom is an aggregate of villages under a centralized rule of a paramount political leader (Oberg 1955:484; Redmond 1998). In other words, chiefdoms are regionally organized societies with a centralized decision-making hierarchy coordinating activities among several village communities (Earle 1991, 1997). Chiefdoms are intermediate-level societies, providing an evolutionary bridge between autonomous societies and bureaucratic states (Earle 1987). For many researchers (Service 1962; Earle 1987; Creamer and Haas 1985; Drennan and Uribe 2007), chiefdoms are different from bands and tribes both in degree and in kind. Chiefdoms are based on the concept of hereditary inequality. In a chiefdom society, if you are the son of a chief, chances are you will become chief no matter how unsuitable you may be, and if you are born a "commoner," your options in life will be narrowly circumscribed, regardless of how able you might be (Wenke and Olszewski 1962; Earle 1987; Creamer and Haas 1985; Drennan and Uribe 2007). These differences in prestige usually correlate with preferential access to wealth. Chiefs and their families can claim the best farmlands or fishing places, as well as more food and more "exotic" items than the families of commoners. In chiefdoms, control over production and exchange of subsistence and wealth creates the basis for political power. Characteristically, the chief operates some kind of redistributive system wherein food, goods, or both are brought together from different sectors of the chiefdom and then distributed according to fixed social rules (Darvill 2002). However, in Hawaii, the role of the chief as a redistributor has been seriously questioned (Earle 1977). In Hawaii, local communities ensured their own subsistence by various means and the chiefs levied tribute from them to finance their own activities (Earle 1977). Although chiefdoms are highly variable, the organization at this scale usually requires a political hierarchy for coordination and decision-making (G. Johnson 1982). Archaeologists generally use the presence and distribution of monumental constructions and prestige goods to document the evolution of chiefly societies (Creamer and Haas 1985).

Taíno Chiefdoms

Many elements of Taíno societies in the northern Caribbean are based on chiefdoms. The Taíno villages were loosely organized into district chiefdoms, each ruled by one of the village chiefs in the district. The district chiefdoms were in turn grouped into regional chiefdoms, each headed by the most prominent district chief (Figure 11.1). The regional boundaries might have been delimited by geographical demarcations. However, the boundaries may have been based on factors outside of geography, such as economic control, military leadership, linguistic, and ethnic affiliations (Wilson 1990). Although chiefs were predominantly men, both men and women were eligible to serve as chiefs, or caciques. Chiefs lived in specially built houses (called *bohíos*), sat on thronelike stools (called *duhos*), were carried around by their servants in litters, and wore insignia of their rank (Rouse 1992). Male caciques were polygamous, and some of their wives were from other communities. Marrying outside one's own village was one way for a cacique to acquire power and cement alliances with neighboring chiefs (Alegría 1997).

Caciques presided over the village in which they lived. They organized the daily activities and were responsible for the storage of surplus commodities, which they kept in buildings constructed for this purpose and redistributed among the villagers as needed (Rouse 1992). The power of the cacique extended to collective production. When Bartholomew Columbus (Christopher's younger brother) demanded gold from the cacique Behecchio of Xaraguá in Hispaniola, the latter replied that he did not have gold, but he could fill several Spanish caravels with cotton (Veloz Maggiolo 1997). The chiefs acted as hosts whenever the villages received visitors, and they were the primary organizers

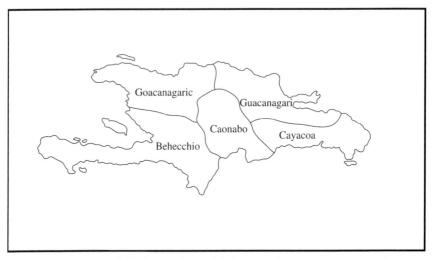

Figure 11.1. Reconstructed chiefdoms in Hispaniola based on the names of caciques, as interpreted by Pierre Charlevoix (1730). (Adapted from Wilson, *Hispaniola*, 110.)

of ceremonial feastings, ball games, and trade relations with outside groups. Clearly, the social organization of the Taínos was ranked, with a small elitist group in control of the society's resources. But there was wealth distribution by chiefs, which may have created stability, peace, and goodwill in the society, leading to the inaccurate, simplistic description of peaceful Arawaks or peaceful Taínos.

Ball Courts and Stone-lined Plazas

Another sign of the Taíno hierarchical social organization throughout much of the northern Caribbean is the presence of ball courts (Figure 11.2) and stone-lined plazas (Rouse 1992). These plazas were probably constructed through the collective efforts of workers who were coordinated by a centralized authority. This level of social organization can be compared to other ranked societies worldwide, such as the Adena and Howell mound builders in eastern North America and the early Polynesians in Tahiti, Hawaii, and Easter Islands (Fagan 2002).

The Taínos were adept at constructing plazas and ball courts, typically composed of earth embankments and stone slabs (Olazagasti 1997). These constructions were related to similar structures throughout South America, Mesoamerica, and southwest North America (Wilson 1990). Sometimes the stone slabs were decorated with carvings of human and animal forms (called petroglyphs). In the Caribbean, ball courts varied in size but generally the courts

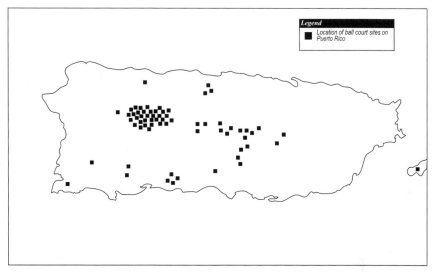

Figure 11.2. Location of ball court sites on Puerto Rico. (Adapted from Wilson, *Hispaniola*, 110.)

were oval or long and narrow rectangles and could have been used either as ball courts or dance grounds (Olazagasti 1997). Of all the stone-lined plazas in the northern Caribbean, probably the most elaborate and specialized complex of ball and dance courts can be found at the Caguana site (also know as Capá) in the mountains northwest of the El Bronce and Tibes sites in Puerto Rico (Rouse 1992) (Figure 11.3). The sides of the central court are lined with vertically placed limestone slabs and granite boulders; its ends are closed with stone pavements. Many of the slabs and boulders are decorated with petroglyphs, which portray zemis (Rouse 1992). At Caguana, the courts were leveled by digging out and terracing the uphill sides.

The ball courts were the sites of public rituals and dances and for the ball game itself (Wilson 1990). In the game, two teams competed in trying to keep a ball from falling to the ground, using any part of their bodies except their hands. The ball game was a venue for interaction and competition between villages and larger polities and apparently had social and political ramifications that exceeded the Spanish observers' understanding (Wilson 1992). Spectators are thought to have observed the dances and games from nearby terraces and from nearby mounds of earth, which were probably constructed for that purpose (Rouse 1992).

Geopolitics and Taíno ball courts were inextricably linked. In Puerto Rico, ball courts were clustered on political boundaries where they served to manage political relations between regional chiefdoms (called *cacicazgos*) (Rodriguez 1995). Such courts have been discovered in the southern Bahamas (Middle

Figure II.3. Aerial view of the Caguana dance and ball courts (looking south-southeast of the Caguana site). (Reproduced from Rouse, *The Taínos*. Photograph by Agamemnon Gus Pantel. Used by permission.)

Caicos) and St. Croix, reflecting the northern and eastern boundaries of the Classic Taínos culture (Keegan 1997; Rouse 1992). Excavated by Shaun Sullivan in the late 1970s, the MC-6 ceremonial–trading center on Middle Caicos has a two-plaza community plan (Figure II.4). This plan is more typical of Classic Taíno settlement, although the pottery at these sites is predominantly Meillacan Ostionoid (Keegan 1997). The site measures 247 m (270 yd) long by 64 m (70 yd) wide, the margins of which are defined by middens that are punctuated by pit features with low lime rock walls (Keegan 1997).

Trade

An important aspect of Taíno chiefdoms that is recoverable archaeologically includes items traded as prestige goods from polity to polity and island to island (Wilson 1990). Trading of exotic items was part of the chiefs' elite exchange network, which helped to build regional alliances among trading partners. Of the many trade goods that were reported in the ethnohistorical accounts, only

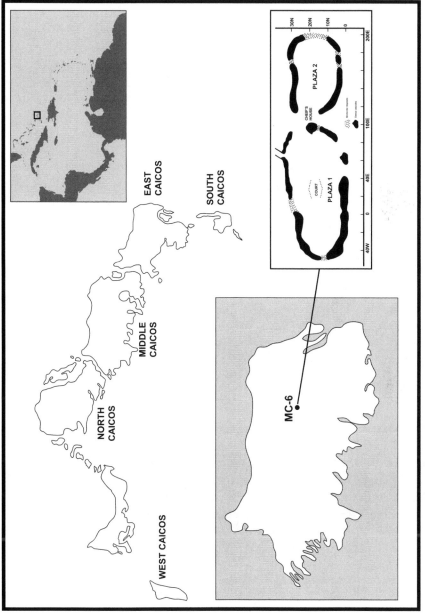

Figure 11.4. Two-plaza site of MC-6 on Middle Caicos.

a few are preserved in archaeological contexts. Ethnohistorical accounts mention such items as parrots, feathers, raw and woven cotton, carved woods, gold, and *guanín* (a gold alloy) (Lovén 1935). The trade objects that are most evident archaeologically are the elaborate ceramics, such as anthropomorphic (or humanlike) and zoomorphic (or animal-like) effigy bottles, and carved stone objects (Wilson 1990). Elaborate ceramics, probably from Hispaniola, appear as trade items in Cuba, Jamaica, Puerto Rico, and the Bahamas (Alegría 1976). They are often marked with repetitive and highly stylized artistic motifs suggesting that the goods possessed a greater and more specific symbolic content than that of goods that simply marked social status. There may have been regular trading contacts between the Taínos and their neighbors in the circum-Caribbean area. The ethnohistorical evidence for contact with Mesoamerica is scant but it does suggest contact between the Taínos and their neighbors in Central America. For example, there is mention in a version of the Popul Vuh (the Mayan creation myth) of a possible attack by Caribbean Indians, and Bernal Díaz del Castillo's history of the conquest of Mexico mentions a Jamaican woman on Cozumel (Wilson 1990). Trading over such long distances was quite possible, given the seaworthiness of native canoes in the Bahamas and Cuba, which Columbus described as being able to comfortably hold 50 to 150 men (Dunn and Kelley 1989). Trade networks were extensive during the Ostionoid period encompassing all of the Greater Antilles and possibly through the Lesser Antilles to mainland South America. Contact with Mesoamerica is further suggested by the similarities in the ball games played both in Mesoamerica and the Greater Antilles (Alegría 1983).

Conclusion

Clearly, the Spaniards did not bring civilization to the northern Caribbean but instead found socially complex native communities scattered throughout the region. These communities were governed by hereditary chiefs who, among other things, managed production and the redistribution of surplus wealth. They also traded with their counterparts throughout the region and coordinated the construction of major architectural monuments.

Conclusion

When Christopher Columbus first arrived in the Caribbean in 1492, he did not find timeless, primitive isolates, but rather socially complex Taíno societies that had already established local, district, and regional chiefdoms and had an impressive network of trading contacts with their Caribbean and circum-Caribbean neighbors. Also of significance is the fact that before the emergence of the Taínos, a diverse collection of native groups had already migrated to the region. Out of these migrations, new indigenous communities were created through cultural evolution as well as through multiple, recursive, and dynamic interactions over thousands of years.

In this book, "Caribbean history" pertains to both the pre- and postcolonial eras. This flies in the face of certain conventions that create artificial boundaries between so-called prehistory and history. Prehistory is usually defined by archaeologists as that portion of human history that extends back some 2.5 million years before the time of written documents and archives (Fagan 1999). History is usually defined as the study of the human experience through documents, which generally has a much shorter time span. Written records go back about five thousand years in western Asia. In the New World, writing began with the advent of Christopher Columbus in 1492. Only during the late eighteenth and early twentieth centuries, when European powers annexed other parts of the world such as sections of Africa and Asia (Fagan 1999), did both writing and written records come into vogue in those territories. The conventional definition of history, which is based exclusively on written records, has demonstrably created false dichotomies between the Western and non-Western world. Past events of the non-Western world have been relegated to the domain of prehistory, irrespective of its much longer time period and irrespective of how much of it has been richly documented through oral traditions and archaeological research. This book argues for a total history, one that embraces the whole of human activity as history, regardless of time periods, ethnicities, or geographical boundaries.

Archaeology is the primary medium through which aspects of Caribbean history are distilled and presented in this book. Whether used in isolation or in combination with ethnography, ethnohistory, and oral history, archaeology is essentially about people. It is about human behaviors, about people's social, economic, and political interactions, about their religious beliefs, burial practices, community organization, settlement patterns, diet, and even about how they perceived and measured time. The archaeologist is a kind of anthropologist concerned primarily not with living societies but with ancient ones (Fagan 1999). And what holds anthropology together is its dogmatic insistence that every aspect of every society—extant or extinct—counts (Thomas 1999). By using a broad range of scientific methods and techniques for studying the past, Caribbean archaeologists study the human societies of the remote and recent past, using the surviving material remains of their cultures to reconstruct their histories. As ongoing archaeological investigations in the Caribbean reveal new and exciting information about the region's past, more traditionally accepted theories and assumptions may be exposed for what they are—myths based on a Eurocentric worldview.

Glossary

amoebic dysentery. Transmitted through contamination of drinking water, it is prevalent in developing nations, although it is occasionally seen in industrialized countries. It is sometimes called "traveler's dysentery" or "Montezuma's revenge." Liver infection and subsequent amoebic abscesses can occur. It is caused mainly by the protozoan *Entamoeba histolytica*.

anthropophagy. Human cannibalism. The word is derived from Greek *anthropos*, "man" and *phagein*, "to eat."

anthropomorphic. Resembling human form or displaying human attributes.

anthropozoomorphic. Bearing both human and animal characteristics or forms.

appliqué. French word meaning "applied." For example, a motif or design made separately, then affixed to a ceramic vessel.

Archaic. A developmental stage characterized by a marine-oriented subsistence followed by a terrestrial hunting-based economy. The absence of pottery was until recently considered a defining characteristic of Archaic peoples. However, evidence of pottery-making among the Casimiroids and Ortoiroids has now invalidated this idea.

assimilation. A process by which a minority group is absorbed into a majority population, during which the minority group takes on the values and norms of the dominant culture.

Barrancoid. The Barrancoid peoples take their name from the site of Barrancas on the banks of the lower Orinoco River in Venezuela. Their culture seems to have developed out of the local Saladoid tradition in Venezuela between 1500 and 1000 B.C. Barrancoid peoples moved northward to the Orinoco river delta, perhaps displacing or bypassing other Saladoid communities as they went, and occupied islands of the Caribbean as far north as Puerto Rico. Like the Saladoids, they cultivated cassava, produced pottery, and lived in villages. The discovery of Barrancoid pottery in Cedrosan

Saladoid sites in Trinidad and Tobago dating to A.D. 350 suggests extensive trade between the Barrancoids and the Saladoids.

bejel. A chronic skin and tissue disease caused by infection by a subspecies of the spirochete *Treponema pallidum.* Previously called endemic syphilis.

Casimiroids. The Casimiroids, named after Casimira in Dominican Republic, probably migrated from Belize in the Yucatán Peninsula and lived between 4000 and 400 B.C. in Cuba and Hispaniola. They made flaked-tools, conical pestles, disks, and daggerlike objects. Evidence now suggests that they were also potters and horticulturalists.

Chican. The Chican subseries, which developed in the Dominican Republic, spread to Puerto Rico and St. Croix, if not to the rest of the Virgin Islands, and strongly influenced the cultures of the northern Leeward Islands. Usually associated with the Classic Taínos, Chican pottery, especially the Boca Chica style, is characterized by more highly polished surfaces and more refined modeled-incisions than the other Ostionoid and Taíno pottery subseries elsewhere in the northern Caribbean.

cognates. Having a common ancestor. For instance, English and Danish are cognate languages, both being Germanic. Every language in the Indo-European language family has lexical items that are cognate with lexical items in another language in the family. Indeed, the Indo-European language family is defined by its cognates: one two three, eins zwei drei, un deux trois, and so on.

cohoba. A hallucinogenic powder made from the seeds of the tree *Anadenanthera peregrina* and inhaled through the nose. The term also refers to the ritual involving the use of this substance. Cohoba was widely practiced by precolonial Amerindian groups throughout the Caribbean and usually involved fasting, dancing, purging, bathing, and chanting.

culture history. An archaeological method by which archaeologists use artifacts to determine the who, when, and where of past cultures, based on the material record. Describing and classifying finds into groups is an important part of culture history, and classification can be done through design styles, geographic distributions, or chronological periods. An excellent example of the application of culture history in Caribbean archaeology is the "series" and "subseries" approach, which relates to "cultures" and "peoples" respectively.

cultural evolution. Describes how cultures and societies have developed over time. Although cultural evolutionary models typically provide an understanding of the relationship between technologies, social structure, the values of a society, and how and why they change with time, they vary as to the extent to which they describe specific mechanisms of variation and social change.

egalitarianism. A sociopolitical system that professes to support the belief that all members of a society are equal, particularly with regard to social, economic, and political rights. Some inequalities in relation to gender, age, and special physical characteristics may be found in egalitarian societies. This can be contrasted to a ranked sociopolitical system where a small elitist group controls most, if not all, of the resources of a society.

Elenan. Subseries of the Ostionoid series that was contemporary with the Ostionan subseries on the western half of Puerto Rico. This subseries was distributed over the eastern half of the island. Two ceramic styles for this subseries have been recognized in eastern Puerto Rico. The earliest is Monserrate (A.D. 600–850), and the other is Santa Elena (A.D. 850–1200). The Monserrate ceramic style is essentially a development from the earlier Cuevas style but without the elaborate decoration, such as polychrome painting. Decoration consisted of red- or black-painted geometric designs and strap handles. In the following Santa Elena period, ceramics are characterized by loss of strap handles, production of mainly bowl forms, the abandonment of painted decoration, and polishing. Modeling and incising became the major ceramic decoration. As with the Ostionan subseries, the larger Elenan Ostionoid subseries sites have associated ball courts. Some sites, like Tibes, have multiple plazas and ball courts. Major sites associated with the Elenan Ostionoid subseries are Tibes, Collores, and El Bronce.

elite exchange. "Gift-giving" among elite groups. Elite exchange, characteristic of Taíno chiefdoms, was designed to build alliances locally and regionally.

ethnohistory. Study of ancient (often non-Western) cultures using evidence from documentary sources and oral traditions, often supplemented with archaeological data.

foraging. Searching for food. Within the science of behavioral ecology it refers to predator-prey interactions.

flaking. Refers to the removal of flakes by striking a core or other objective piece, such as a partially formed tool with a hammer or percussor. The object can also be struck against a stationary anvil-stone, known as bipolar percussion. Percussors are traditionally either a stone cobble or pebble, often referred to as a hammerstone, or a billet made of bone, antler, or wood. Often, flakes are struck from a core using a punch, in which case the percussor never actually makes contact with the objective piece. This technique is referred to as indirect percussion.

griddle. A flat ceramic plate used for baking manioc as the final stage in the process of detoxifying it for human consumption. The presence of griddles on an archaeological site suggests that manioc was cultivated and processed by the native inhabitants. Griddles are also called burens.

grinding. Simple manual abrasion, as in rubbing an ax on sandstone to produce a ground cutting edge.

horticulture. The culture of growing garden plants. Increasingly, archaeologists are making little or no distinction between horticulture and what is generally described as agriculture.

Island-Caribs. The Island-Caribs appear to have been late arrivals in the Caribbean from South America perhaps around A.D. 1450. They colonized the Windward Islands of Dominica, Martinique, St. Vincent, Grenada and Guadeloupe, as well as Tobago and the northern section of Trinidad. Island-Caribs, Kalinago, or Kalina are names often given to the Caribs inhabiting the Windward Islands when the Europeans arrived, in order to differentiate them from the mainland Caribs of South America.

lapidary. Literally, means "concerned with stones." A lapidary is an artisan who practices the craft of working, forming, and finishing stone, mineral, gemstones, and other suitably durable materials (e.g., amber, shell, jet, pearl, copal, coral, horn, and bone, as well as glass and other synthetics) into functional, decorative, or wearable items (e.g., cameos, cabochons, and more complex faceted designs). Native groups such as the Saladoids practiced lapidary trade, which is the trading of such items.

Lucayan. Indigenous inhabitants of the Bahamas and Turks and Caicos Islands. The Lucayans shared a common ancestry with the Taínos of the Greater Antilles through the Ostionoid peoples who originally settled the islands between A.D.600 and A.D.1200. The term "Lucayan" is an anglicized form of the Spanish name for Las Islas de Los Lucayos.

lug. A projecting piece that is used to lift or support or turn something.

mano. A cylindrical shaped grinding stone used in the hand often in conjunction with a smooth metate. It is used for grinding vegetable material such as maize, seeds, nuts, and pigments.

Meillacan. A subseries of the Ostionoid cultural tradition, which succeeded the Ostiones (Ostionan) people in the Cibao valley of northern Hispaniola. About A.D. 800, the Meillacan people moved into Jamaica and Cuba, following the trail of their Ostiones forebears. The Meillacan people made unpainted pottery, often decorated with rectilinear incisions, crosshatched designs, punctuations, appliqué clay ridges, and small geometric and zoomorphic lugs.

metate. The base or lower grinding stone of a two-part mill for preparing plant food. The upper, movable stone is called a mano. Found in many shapes and sizes, they may be made from any coarse-grained rock that will work well as an abrasive surface.

midden. Refuse heaps often consisting of large accumulations of shells and other food remains, together with fragments of pottery or artifacts of stone and bone.

Ortoiroids. Named after the site of Ortoire in east Trinidad, people of the

Ortoiroid culture arrived in the Caribbean in 5000 B.C. and disappeared around 200 B.C. The earliest Ortoiroid site is Banwari Trace in south Trinidad. Ortoiroid sites are typically dominated by shell middens composed of fresh- and seawater species used mainly for food. Artifacts include bone spear points and barbs as well as perforated animal teeth, choppers, hammerstones, metates, manos, and pestles. There is evidence from the northern Lesser Antilles and Puerto Rico that the Ortoiroids, like the Casimiroids, engaged in pottery-making and horticulture.

Ostionan. The Ostiones or Ostionan is recognized as one of the several variations of the more inclusive Ostionoid Taíno culture in the northern Caribbean. They colonized Cuba and Hispaniola and appear to have been the first human settlers to colonize Jamaica, around A.D. 600. These people made Ostionan Ostionoid pottery, also called redware. The red serves primarily as a background covering part or all of the vessel surface instead of delineating it. The pottery is thin, hard, and smooth surfaced.

Other. A term used in anthropology in relation to subordinate groups in society such as minorities and women.

Palmetto. Pottery series made by the Lucayans of the Bahamas. Palmetto pottery is distributed throughout both parts of the archipelago, the Turks, and the Bahama islands. It is technologically inferior to the rest of the Ostionoid pottery in the northern Caribbean, primarily because of the poor quality of the clay in the Bahamian archipelago. Thick, crude, and mostly shell-tempered, Palmetto pottery is so friable that it breaks into tiny sherds. Similar to the Meillacan styles, this pottery type has examples of appliqué work and punctuation.

peccary. A piglike mammal of the genus *Tayassu* of North and South America.

pecking. A method of shaping the surface of natural stones to fashion tools, modify the form of the stone, or create patterns or designs of various sorts. It involves hitting the surface of the stone to be fashioned in a controlled way using a harder stone of appropriate size (a hammerstone) thereby crushing the surface of softer stone to a powder and so removing small portions at each blow.

perimortem. Occurring at the time of death.

pestle. A club-shaped tool used for crushing or pounding material in a mortar.

pinta. A rare tropical skin disease caused by *Treponema carateum,* which is related to the bacterium that causes syphilis.

polity. A politically organized unit.

projectile points. Stone, bone, or metal points made to strengthen the tip of a spear or arrow. The point is usually made out of a different material from the shaft.

Saladoid. The Ceramic-age people who moved into the Caribbean in the last

centuries B.C. have come to be known as the Saladoids, after the archaeological site Saladero in Venezuela at which their characteristic pottery was
found. This ceramic-making group migrated from Trinidad/Venezuela to
the Leeward Islands, U.S. Virgin Islands (St. Thomas, St. Croix, and St.
John), and eastern Puerto Rico. Their pottery styles can be divided into two
groups: the Cedros style pottery (250 B.C.–A.D. 1) and the Palo Seco complex (A.D. 1–A.D. 650).

sigmoid. Shaped like the letter S.

Suazan Troumassoids. Taking their name from the Savanne Suazey site on
Grenada, the Suazey people displayed a preference for sandy beaches and
mangrove swamps. Although some texts refer to them as Suazoids, Caribbean archaeologists are increasingly referring to them as Suazan Troumassoids because their artifacts are too similar to those of earlier Troumassoid
groups to be given a completely different cultural classification. The group
flourished in the Lesser Antilles from about A.D. 1000 to around 1450.

Taínos. Indigenous Amerindian inhabitants of the northern Caribbean whom
Columbus encountered when he arrived in 1492. The Taínos evolved from
the Ostionoid peoples and inhabited the Caribbean from A.D. 1200 to
1500.

transculturation. Coined by Fernando Ortiz in 1947, transculturation is the
constant interaction between two or more cultural components to uninten-
tionally create a third cultural identity. Although subordinate groups cannot control what emanates from the dominant culture, they do determine
in varying degrees what they absorb into their own cultures and what they
use it for.

vomit spatula. Object that precolonial Amerindians thrust down their throats
to induce vomiting as a means of purifying themselves before ritual activities.

world-system theory. Originally formulated by Immanuel Wallerstein, it describes a world system characterized by mechanisms that bring about a redistribution of resources from the *periphery* to the *core.* In his terminology,
the core is the developed, industrialized, democratic part of the world, which
economically exploits the poor, raw materials–exporting, less-developed
countries called the periphery.

Xaraguá. Regional chiefdom in the southwestern part of Hispaniola, ruled by
Behecchio.

zoomorphic. Representing or resembling animal forms.

References Cited

Acevedo-Rodríguez, P., and collaborators

1996   Flora of St. John, U.S. Virgin Islands. *Memoirs of the New York Botanical Garden* 78:1–581.

Alegría, Ricardo E.

1976   Las relaciones entre los Taínos de Puerto Rico y los se la Española. *Boletín del Instituto Montecristeño de Arqueología* 2.

1981   El uso de la terminologia ethno-históric para designer las culturas aborigines de las Antillas. Cuadernos Prehispánicas, Seminario de Historia de America, University of Valladolid.

1983   *Ball Courts and Ceremonial Stone-lined Plazas in the West Indies.* Yale University Press.

1997   An Introduction to Taíno Culture and History. In *Taíno: Pre-Columbian Art and Culture from the Caribbean,* edited by Fatima Bercht, Estrellita Brodsky, John Alan Farmer, and Dicey Taylor, pp. 18–33. Monacelli Press.

Allaire, Louis

1984   A Reconstruction of Early Historical Island Carib Pottery. *Southeastern Archaeology* 3 (2) (Winter 1984):121–33.

1990   Prehistoric Taíno Interaction with the Lesser Antilles: The View from Martinique, F.W.I. Paper presented at the Fifty-fifth Annual Meeting of the Society for American Archaeology, Las Vegas, Nevada, April 18–22.

1991   Understanding Suazey. In *Proceedings of the Thirteenth Congress of the International Association for Caribbean Archaeology,* edited by J. B. Haviser and E. N. Ayubi, pp. 715–28. Curaçao.

1997   The Lesser Antilles before Columbus. In *The Indigenous People of the Caribbean,* edited by Samuel Wilson, pp. 20–28. University Press of Florida.

Allsworth-Jones, Philip, and Michiel Kappers

2007   Stewart Castle and Retreat, Jamaica: Results of a New Digital Mapping Survey. In *Proceedings of the Twenty-First Congress of the International Association for Caribbean Archaeology,* pp. 91–97, edited by Basil Reid, Henri Petitjean Roget, and Antonio Curet. University of the West Indies, School of Continuing Studies, St. Augustine, Trinidad.

Angulo, C.

1992   *Isla de Cuba, pintoresca, histórica, política, mercantile e industrial.* Recuerdos y
        apuntes de los épocas. Boix, Madrid.

Arens, William

1979   *The Man-Eating Myth.* Oxford University Press.

Ashdown, Peter, and Francis Humphreys

1988   *Caribbean Revision History for CXC.* Macmillan Caribbean.

Beckles, Hilary M.

1992   Kalinago (Carib) Resistance to European Colonization of the Caribbean.
        Caribbean Quarterly 38 (2–3):1–14.

Bennett, J. P.

1989   *An Arawak-English Dictionary.* Walter Roth Museum of Anthropology,
        Guyana.

Berkhofer, Robert F., Jr.

1979   *The White Man's Indian.* Vintage Books.

Birmingham, David

2000   *Trade and Empire in the Atlantic, 1400–1600* Introductions to History Series.
        Routledge.

Bischof, Barbie, Elizabeth Rowe, Arthur J. Mariano, and Edward H. Ryan

2004   The North Equatorial Current. Ocean Surface Currents. *http://oceancurrents.
        rsmas.miami.edu/atlantic/north-equatorial.html*, accessed on July 7, 2008.

Black, Clinton V.

1973   *History of Jamaica.* William Collins and Sangster.

1983   *A New History of Jamaica.* William Collins and Sangster.

Bogucki, Peter

1999   Early Agricultural Societies. *Companion Encyclopedia of Archaeology,* edited
        by Graeme Baker, pp. 839–69, vol. 2. Routledge.

Boomert, Arie

1986   The Cayo Complex of St. Vincent: Ethnohistorical and Archaeological
        Aspects of the Islands-Carib Problem. *Anthropologica* 66:3–68.

2000   *Trinidad and Tobago and the Lower Orinoco Interaction Sphere: An
        Archaeological/Ethnohistorical Study.* Cairi Publications.

2003   Agricultural Societies in the Continental Caribbean. In *General History of
        the Caribbean,* edited by Jalil Sued Badillo, pp. 134–94, vol. 1. Autochthonous
        Societies, UNESCO Publishing.

Brill, R. H., I. L. Barnes, S. S. C. Tong, and M. J. Murtaugh

1987   Laboratory Studies of Some European Artifacts Excavated on San Salvador
        Island. In *Proceedings of the First Conference, Columbus and His World,* edited
        by D. T. Gerace, pp. 97–102. CCFL Bahamian Field Station, Fort Lauder-
        dale.

Brumfiel, Elizabeth M.

1992   Distinguished Lecture in Archaeology: Breaking and Entering the
        Ecosystem—Gender, Class, and Faction Steal the Show. *American
        Anthropologist* 94:551–65.

Bryan, Patrick

1992   Spanish Jamaica. *Caribbean Quarterly* 38 (2–3):21–31.

Buckridge, Steve O.

2004   *Language of Dress: Resistance and Accommodation in Jamaica, 1750–1890.* University of West Indies Press.

Bullen, Ripley P.

1964   The Archaeology of Grenada. *Contributions of the Florida State Museum* 11.

1965   Archaeological Chronology of Grenada. *American Antiquity* 31 (2) pt. 1 (Oct. 1965), pp. 237–41, www.jstor.org/cgi-bin/jstor/printpage/00027316/di021307/02p0047r/0.pdf?backcontext=page&dowhat=Acrobat&config=jstor&userID=401c8702@uwi.tt/01c0a834710050ic13f69&0.pdf, accessed on March 10, 2008.

Bushnell, G. H. S.

1948   *Handbook of South American Indians.* Smithsonian Institution, Bureau of American Ethnology. 3:535–41.

Callaghan, Richard T.

1990   Mainland Origins of the Pre-Ceramic Cultures of the Greater Antilles. Ph.D. dissertation, University of Calgary.

1995   Antillean Cultural Contacts with Mainland Region as a Navigation Problem. In *Proceedings of the Fifteenth International Congress for Caribbean Archaeology,* edited by R. E. Alegría and M. Rodríguez, pp. 181–90. Centro de Estudios Avanzados de Puerto Rico y el Caribe, San Juan.

2001   Ceramic Age Seafaring and Interaction Potential in the Antilles: A Computer Simulation. *Current Anthropology* 42 (2) (Nov. 2):308–12.

2007   Survival of a Traditional Carib Watercraft Design Element. In *Proceedings of the Twenty-First Congress of the International Association for Caribbean Archaeology,* edited by Basil Reid, Henri Petitjean Roget, and Antonio Curet, pp. 739–46. School of Continuing Studies, University of the West Indies, St. Augustine, Trinidad.

Cameron, C. E., C. Castro, S. A. Lukehart, and W. C. Van Voorhis

1999   Sequence Conservation of Glycerophosphodiester Phosphodiesterase among *Treponema pallidum* Strains. *Infection and Immunity* 67(6):3168–70.

Carlin, Eithne B., and Jacques Arends (editors)

2002   *Atlas of the Languages of Suriname.* KITLV Press.

Cauchois, Mickaelle-Hinanui

2002   Dryland Horticulture in Maupiti: An Ethnoarchaeological Study. *Asian Perspectives: The Journal of Archaeology for Asia and Pacific,* vol. 41, www.questia.com/googleScholar.qst;jsessionid=H2kGB8hHJQmF5gSJnLpdpvdthgbf1V97nJXmy6fkD21TJdVFcnXp!191140884?docId=5000605687, accessed on February 22, 2008.

Centurion-Lara, A., C. Godornes, C. Castro, W. C. Van Voorhis, and S. A. Lukehart

2000   The tprK Gene Is Heterogeneous among *Treponema palladium* Strains and Has Multiple Alleles. *Infection and Immunity* 68:824–31.

Chanlatte Baik, L. A.

1981   *La Hueca y Sorcé (Vieques, Puerto Rico): Primeras migraciones agroalfareras an-tillanas.* Published by the author, Santo Domingo, Dominican Republic.

1986   Cultura Ostionoide: Un desarrollo agroalfarero antillano. *Homines* 10:1–40.

Chanlatte Baik, L. A., and Y. M. Narganes Storde

1983   *Vieques-Puerto Rico: Asiento de una nueva cultura aborigen antillana.* Published by the authors, Santo Domingo, Dominican Republic.

1985   Asentamiento poblacional Agro-I, complejo cultural La Hueca, Vieques, Puerto Rico. In *Proceedings of the Tenth International Congress for the Study of the Pre-Columbian Cultures of the Lesser Antilles,* edited by A. Allaire, pp. 225–50. Centre de Reserches Caraïbes, Université de Montreal, Montreal.

1986   *Proceso y desarrolo de los primeros pobladores de Puerto Rico y las Antillas.* Published by the authors, Santo Domingo, Dominican Republic.

1990   *La nueva arqueología de Puerto Rico (su proyección en las Antillas).* Taller.

Claypole, William, and John Robottom

2001   *Caribbean Story: Book 2.* Pearson Schools.

2006   *Caribbean Story: Book 1.* Carlong Publishers (Caribbean).

Cody, A.

1995   Kalinago Alliance Networks. In *Proceedings of the Fifteenth International Congress for Caribbean Archaeology,* edited by R. Alegría and M. Rodríguez, pp. 311–26. Centro de Estudios Avanzados de Puerto Rico y el Caribe, San Juan.

Creamer, Winifred, and J. Haas

1985   Tribes vs. Chiefdoms in Lower Central America. *American Antiquity* 50:738–54.

Crosby, Alfred W.

1986   *Ecological Imperialism: The Biological Expansion of Europe, 900–1900.* London.

2003   *Biological and Cultural Consequences of 1492.* Greenwood Press.

Curet, L. Antonio

1992   The Development of Chiefdoms in the Greater Antilles: A Regional Study of the Valley of Maunabo, Puerto Rico. Ph.D. dissertation, Department of Anthropology, Arizona State University, Tempe.

1996   Ideology, Chiefly Power, and Material Culture: An Example from the Greater Antilles. *Latin American Antiquity* 7.

2005   *Caribbean Paleodemography.* University of Alabama Press.

Dacal Moure, R., and M. Rivero de la Calle

1984   *Arqueología aborigen de Cuba.* Editorial Gente Nueva.

1997   *Art and Archaeology of Pre-Columbian Cuba.* University of Pittsburgh Press.

Darvill, Timothy

2002   *The Concise Oxford Dictionary of Archaeology.* Oxford University Press.

Davis, D. D.

1982   Archaic Settlement and Resource Exploitation in the Lesser Antilles: Pre-liminary Information from Antigua. *Caribbean Journal of Science* 17:107–22.

de Albuquerque, Martim

1974　*Notes and Queries.* Oxford University Press.

Degusta, David

1999　Fijian Cannibalism: Osteological Evidence from Navatu. *American Journal of Physical Anthropology* 110:215–41.

Desowitz, Robert S.

1997　*Who Gave Pinta to the Santa Maria: Torrid Diseases in a Temperate World.* W. W. Norton.

Digerfeldt, G., and M. D. Hendry

1987　An 8000 Year Holocene Sea-level Record from Jamaica: Implications for Interpretation of Caribbean Reef and Coastal History. *Coral Reefs* 5(4):165–69.

Dobres, Marcia-Anne, and John E. Robb (editors)

2000　*Agency in Archaeology.* Routledge.

Dookhan, Isaac

2006　*A Pre-Emancipation History of the West Indies.* Longman Publishing for the Caribbean.

Douglas, Nik

1991　Recent Amerindian Finds on Anguilla. In *Proceedings of the Thirteenth International Congress for Caribbean Archaeology,* pp. 576–88, Archaeological-Anthropological Institute of the Netherland Antilles, Willemstad.

Drennan, R. D., and C. A. Uribe (editors)

2007　*Chiefdoms in the Americas.* University Press of America.

Drewett, Peter

1991　*Prehistoric Barbados.* Archetype Publications; Institute of Archaeology, University College London.

1999　*Field Archaeology: An Introduction.* UCL Press, Taylor and Francis Group.

Dunn, O., and J. E. Kelley Jr. (editors)

1989　*The Diario of Christopher Columbus's First Voyage to America, 1492–1493.* Abstracted by Bartolomé de las Casas. University of Oklahoma Press.

Earle, Timothy

1987　Chiefdoms in Archaeological and Ethnohistorical Perspectives. *Annual Review of Anthropology* 16:279–308.

1991　*Chiefdoms, Power, Economy, and Ideology.* Cambridge University Press.

1997　*How Chiefs Come to Power.* Stanford University Press.

Evans-Pritchard, E.

1939　Nuer Time-reckoning. *Africa: Journal of the International African Institute* 12:189–216.

Fagan, Brian

1999　*World Prehistory: A Brief Introduction.* 4th ed. Longman.

2002　*World Prehistory: A Brief Introduction.* 5th ed. Prentice-Hall.

2005　*World Prehistory: A Brief Introduction.* 6th ed. Pearson Prentice-Hall.

Farr, S.

1995　Gender and Ethnogenesis in the Early Colonial Lesser Antilles. In *Proceed-*

ings of the Fifteenth International Congress for Caribbean Archaeology, edited by R. Alegría and M. Rodríguez, pp. 367–76. Centro de Estudios Avanzados de Puerto Rico y el Caribe, San Juan.

Fernandez-Jalvo, Y., J. C. Diez, I. Caceres, and J. Rosell
1999   Human Cannibalism in the Early Pleistocene of Europe (Gran Dolina, Sierra de Atapuerca, Burgos, Spain). *Journal of Human Evolution* 37:591–622.

Ford, J.
1969   *A Comparison of Formative Cultures in the Americas. Diffusion or the Physic Unity of Mankind.* Smithsonian Institution, Washington, D.C.

Foster, H. Thomas, II
2003   Dynamic Optimization of Horticulture among the Muscogee Creek Indians of the Southeastern United States. *Journal of Anthropological Archaeology* 22 (4):411–24, www.sciencedirect.com/science?_ob=ArticleURL&_udi=B6WH6-49D2BPH-1&_user=3237081&_rdoc=1&_fmt=&_orig=search&_sort=d&view=c&_acct=C000060084&_version=1&_urlVersion=0&_userid=3237081&md5=d963d4bdab8bc2e20eb3f5f47aed5579, accessed on February 22, 2008.

Gell, Alfred
1996   *The Anthropology of Time.* Berg.

Gilmore, John, Beryl M. Allen, Dian McCallum, and Romila Ramdeen
2003   *Empires and Conquest.* Longman Publishing for the Caribbean.

González, Nancie
1988   *Sojourners of the Caribbean: Ethnogenesis and Ethnohistory of the Garifuna.* University of Illinois Press.

Gosden, Christopher
1994   *Social Being and Time.* Blackwell.

Granberry, Julian
1993   The People Who Discovered Columbus: The Prehistory of the Bahamas: A Review and Commentary. *Florida Anthropologist* 46:56–60.

Granberry, Julian, and Gary S. Vescelius
2004   *Languages of the Pre-Columbian Antilles.* University of Alabama Press.

Griffin, P. B.
1984   Forager Resource and Land Use in the Humid Tropics: The Agta of Northeastern Luzon, the Philippines. In *Past and Present in Hunter Gatherer Studies,* edited by C. Schrire, pp. 95–121. Academic Press.

Harrington, M. R.
1921   *Cuba before Columbus.* Indian Notes and Monographs. Part 1, vol. 2. National Museum of the American Indian.

Harris, Peter
1971   Banwari Trace: Preliminary Report on a Pre-Ceramic Site in Trinidad, West Indies. In *Trinidad and Tobago Historical Society (S. Sec.)* Point-à-Pierre.

Hastrup, K.
1992   *Other Histories.* Routledge.

Haviser, Jay B.

1997   Settlement Strategies in the Early Ceramic Age. In *The Indigenous People of the Caribbean*, edited by S. Wilson, pp. 57–69. University Press of Florida.

Henige, David

1991   *In Search of Columbus: The Sources for the First Voyage.* University of Arizona Press.

Hides, S.

1996   The Genealogy of Material Culture and Cultural Identity. In *Cultural Identity and Archaeology: The Construction of European Communities*, edited by P. Graves-Brown, S. Jones, and C. Gamble, pp. 25–47. Routledge.

Hock, Hans Henrich

1986   *Principles of Historical Linguistics.* Mouton de Gruyter.

Hoffman, C. A., Jr.

1987a   Archaeological Investigations at the Long Bay Site, San Salvador, Bahamas. In *Proceedings of the First San Salvador Conference, Columbus and His World*, edited by D. T. Gerace, pp. 97–102. CCFL Bahamian Field Station, Fort Lauderdale.

1987b   The Long Bay Site, San Salvador. *American Archaeology* 6:97–102.

Hofman, Corrine, and M. L. P. Hoogland

1991   The Late Prehistory of Saba, Netherlands, Antilles. In *Thirteenth International Congress for Caribbean Archaeology*, pp. 477–92, Archaeological-Anthropological Institute of the Netherland Antilles, Willemstad.

Hofman, Corrine L., and M. L. P. Hoogland (editors)

1999   *Archaeological Investigations on St. Martin, 1993: The Sites of Norman Estate, Hope Estate, Anse de Peres.* Direction Régionale des Affaires Culturelles de Guadeloupe, Service Régionale de l'Archéologie, Basse-Terre, Guadeloupe.

Hofman, Corrine, L., Menno L. P. Hoogland, Alistair Bright, and William Keegan

2007   Insular Caribbean Society: A Dynamic Relationship between People, Goods, and Ideas during the Pre-Colonial Times. Manuscript.

Hulme, Peter

1986   *Colonial Encounters: Europe and the Native Caribbean, 1492–1797.* Methuen.

1993   Making Sense of the Native Caribbean. *New West Indian Guide* 67 (3–4):189–220.

Hung, Ulloa

2005   Early Ceramics in the Caribbean. In *Dialogues in Cuban Archaeology*, edited by L. Antonio Curet, Shannon Lee Dawdy, and Gabino La Rosa Corzo, pp. 103–24. University of Alabama Press.

Hunnius, Tanya E. von, Charlotte A. Roberts, Anthea Boyston, and Shelley R. Saunders

2005   Histological Identification of Syphilis in Pre-Columbian England. *American Journal of Physical Anthropology* 129 (4) 559–66, www3.interscience.wiley.com/cgi-bin/abstract/112211587/ABSTRACT, accessed on February 16, 2008.

Ingold, W. K.

1984   Time, Social Relationships, and the Exploitation of Animals: Anthropo-
        logical Reflections on Prehistory. In *Animals and Archaeology*, vol. 3, *Early
        Herders and Their Flocks,* edited by J. Clutton-Brock and C. Grigson. British
        Archaeological Reports, International Series, 202:3–12.

Johnson, Christopher

2003   *Claude Lévi-Strauss: The Formative Years.* Cambridge University Press.

Johnson, Gregory

1982   Organizational Structure and Scalar Stress. In *Theory and Explanation in Ar-
        chaeology,* edited by C. Renfrew, M. Rowlands, and B. Seagrave, pp. 389–42.
        Academic Press.

Jones, Siân

1997   *The Archaeology of Ethnicity.* Routledge.

Jouravleva, I.

2002   Origen de la alfarería de las communidades protoagroalfareras de la región
        central de Cuba. *El Caribe Arqueológico* 6:35–43.

Keegan, William F.

1948   The West Indies: An Introduction: The Ciboney, the Arawak, the Carib.
        In *Handbook of South American Indians,* vol. 3, edited by Julian Steward,
        pp. 495–565. Bureau of American Ethnology.

1987   Diffusion of Maize from South America: The Antillean Connection Re-
        constructed. In *Emergent Horticultural Economies of the Eastern Woodlands,*
        edited by W. F. Keegan, pp. 373–79. Southern Illinois University, Center for
        Archaeological Investigations.

1992   *The People Who Discovered Columbus: The Prehistory of the Bahamas.* Univer-
        sity Press of Florida.

1994   West Indian Archaeology. 1. Overview and Foragers. *Journal of Archaeological
        Research* 2 (3):255–83.

1995   Modeling Dispersal in the Prehistoric West Indies. *World Archaeology*
        26:400–420.

1996a   West Indian Archaeology. 2. After Columbus. *Journal of Archaeological Re-
        search* 4 (4):265–94.

1996b   Columbus Was a Cannibal: Myth and the First Encounters. In *The Lesser
        Antilles in the Age of European Expansion,* edited by Robert L. Paquette and
        Stanley L. Engerman, pp. 17–32. University Press of Florida.

1997   *Bahamian Archaeology: Life in the Bahamas and the Turks and Caicos before
        Columbus.* Media Publishing, Nassau.

2000   West Indian Archaeology. 3. Ceramic Age. *Journal of Archaeological Research* 8
        (2):135–67.

Keegan, William F., and Reniel Rodríguez Ramos

2007   Archaic Origins of the Classic Taínos. In *Proceedings of the Twenty-first
        Congress of the International Association for Caribbean Archaeology,* edited
        by Basil Reid, Henri Petitjean Roget, and Antonio Curet, pp. 211–17.

School of Continuing Studies, University of the West Indies, St. Augustine, Trinidad.

Lalueza-Fox, C., M. T. P. Gilbert, A. J. Martinez-Fuentes, F. Calafell, and J. Bertranpetit

2003   Mitochondrial DNA from Pre-Columbian Ciboneys from Cuba and the Prehistoric Colonization of the Caribbean. *American Journal of Physical Anthropology* 121 (2):97–108.

Lee, Richard, and Richard Daly (editors)

2004   *The Cambridge Encyclopedia of Hunters and Gatherers.* Cambridge University Press.

Lovén, Sven

1935   *Origins of the Tainan Culture, West Indies.* Elanders Bokfryckeri Akfiebolog.

McGregor, Douglas D.

2007   New World Disorder. In *American Scientist,* www.Americanscientist.org/template/BookReviewTypeDetail/assetid/28654;jsessionid=baa9, accessed on May 8, 2007.

Michener, James

1988   *Caribbean.* Random House.

Miller, Daniel, and Christopher Tilley

1984   *Ideology, Power, and Prehistory.* Cambridge University Press.

Munn, Nancy

1992   The Cultural Anthropology of Time: A Critical Essay. *Annual Review of Anthropology* 21:93–123.

Murphy, A. Reg, David J. Hozjan, Christy N. de Mille, and Alfred A. Levinson

2000   Pre-Columbian Gems and Ornamental Materials from Antigua, West Indies. *Gems and Gemology* 36 (3):234–45.

Myers, Robert A.

1984   Island Carib Cannibalism. *New West Indian Guide* 158:147–84.

Newsom, Lee Ann

1993   Native West Indian Plant Use. Ph.D. dissertation, Department of Anthropology, University of Florida, Gainesville.

Newson, Linda A.

1976   *Aboriginal and Spanish Colonial Trinidad: A Study in Culture Contact.* Academic Press.

Noble, Kingsley G.

1965   *Proto-Arawakan and Its Descendants.* Indiana University.

Olazagasti, Ignacio

1997   The Material Culture of the Taíno Indians. In *The Indigenous People of the Caribbean,* edited by Samuel Wilson, pp. 131–39. University Press of Florida.

Oliver, J. R.

1999   The "La Hueca Problem" in Puerto Rico and the Caribbean: Old Problems, New Perspectives, Possible Solutions. In *Archaeological Investigations on*

St. Martin (Lesser Antilles), edited by C. L. Hofman and M. L. P. Hoogland, pp. 253–97. Faculty of Archaeology, Leiden University, Netherlands.

Olsen, Fred

1974　*On the Trail of the Arawaks.* Civilization of the American Indian Series, vol. 129. University of Oklahoma Press.

Pagán Jiménez, Jaime R., Miguel Rodríguez, Luis A. Chanlatte, and Yvonne Narganes

2005　La temprana introducción y uso de algunas plantas domésticas, silvestres y cultivos en Las Antillas precolombinas. *Diálogo Antropológico* 3(10):1–27.

Pearsall, D.

1989　*Paleoethnobotany: A Handbook of Procedures.* Academic Press.

Persons, A. Brooke

2007　Reconstructing the Guanahatabeys of Western Cuba. In *Proceedings of the Twenty-first Congress of the International Association for Caribbean Archaeology,* edited by Basil Reid, Antonio Curet, and Petitjean Roget, pp. 243–51. School of Continuing Studies, University of the West Indies, St. Augustine, Trinidad.

Petersen, James B.

1996　Archaeology of Trants, Montserrat. Part 3. Chronological and Settlement Data. *Annals of the Carnegie Museum* 63:323–61.

Peterson, J. T.

1978a　Risk and Agricultural Intensification during the Formative Period in the Northern Basin of Mexico. *American Anthropologist* 89:596–616.

1978b　Hunter-Gatherer/Farmer Exchange. *American Anthropologist* 80:335–51.

Piperno, Dolores R., and Deborah M. Pearsall (editors)

1998　*The Origins of Agriculture in the Lowland Neotropics.* Academic Press, San Diego.

Powell, Mary Lucas, and Della Collins Cook

2005　Introduction in *The Myth of Syphilis,* edited by Mary Lucas Powell and Della Collins Cook, pp. 1–8. University Press of Florida.

Reid, Basil A.

1994　Taínos Not Arawaks: The Indigenous Peoples of Jamaica and the Greater Antilles. *Caribbean Geography* 5 (1):67–71.

2003　*Archaeological Surveys and Excavation of Lot 13 of Marianne Estate, Blanchisseuse, Trinidad (July–August 2003).* Conducted for Mr. Joseph Elias, Nagib Elias and Sons Limited, Port of Spain, Trinidad. Department of History, University of the West Indies, St. Augustine, Trinidad.

2004　Reconstructing the Saladoid Religion in Trinidad and Tobago. *Journal of Caribbean History* 38 (2):243–78.

2005a　*Archaeological Excavations of Lover's Retreat (TOB-69), Tobago (Phases 2 & 3), Final Report.* Conducted for Island Investment Limited (May 2005).

2005b　Caribs Did Not Eat Humans. *Newsday* Sunday, April 17, 2005, 23–25.

2005c　UWI Brings World Archaeology Conference to TT. UWIToday, University of the West Indies, St. Augustine, March 20, 2005. *http://sta.uwi.edu/uwitoday/2005/march/iacaconf.asp*, accessed on July 9, 2008.

2006   Passing of a Pioneer Researcher in Caribbean Archaeology. *UWItoday*, Sunday, March 12, 2006, http://sta.uwi.edu/uwiToday/2006/March/birouse.asp, accessed on July 20, 2007.

Rice, Prudence

2006   *Pottery Analysis: A Sourcebook.* University of Chicago Press.

Rímoli, R. O., and J. Nadal

1980   Cerámica temprana de Hondorus del Oeste. *Boletín del Museo del Hombre Dominicano* 15:17–79.

Rodríguez, Miguel A.

1995   Centros ceremoniales indígenas en Puerto Rico. In *Proceedings of the Fifteenth International Congress for Caribbean Archaeology,* edited by R. E. Alegría and M. Rodríguez., pp. 27–44. Centro de Estudios Avanzados de Puerto Rico y el Caribe, San Juan.

1997   Religious Beliefs of the Saladoid People. In *The Indigenous Peoples,* edited by Samuel Wilson, pp. 80–87. University Press of Florida.

Rodríguez Ramos, Reniel

2002a   Dinámicas de intercambio en el Puerto Rico prehispánico. *El Caribe arqueológico* 6:16–22.

2002b   Una perspectiva diacrónica de la explotación del pedernal en Puerto Rico. *Boletín del Museo del Hombre Dominicano* 32:167–92.

2007   Puerto Rican Precolonial History Etched in Stone. Ph.D. dissertation, Department of Anthropology, University of Florida, Gainesville.

Rogonzinki, Jan

2000   *A Brief History of the Caribbean: From the Arawak and Carib to the Present.* Penguin Group.

Rose, Mark

1997   Origins of Syphilis. *Archaeology* 50 (1) (Jan.–Feb.), www.archaeology. org/9701/newsbriefs/syphilis.html, accessed on August 9, 2007.

Rossen, Jack, and Tom D. Dillehay.

2001   Bone Cutting, Placement, and Cannibalism? Middle Preceramic Mortuary Patterns of Nanchoc, Northern Peru. *Chungará (Arica):*33 (1).

Rothschild, Bruce M.

2005   History of Syphilis. *Clinical Infectious Diseases* 40:1454–63, www.journals. uchicago.edu/doi/abs/10.1086/429626, accessed on February 16, 2008.

Rothschild, Bruce M., Fernando Luna Calderon, Alfredo Coppa, and Christine Rothschild

2000   First European Exposure to Syphilis: The Dominican Republic at the Time of Columbian Contact. *Clinical Infectious Diseases* 31 (Oct.):936–41.

Rouse, Irving

1941   *Culture of Ft. Liberté Region, Haiti.* Yale University.

1952   Porto Rican Prehistory: Excavations in the Interior, South, and East,

Chronological Implications. Scientific Survey of Porto Rico and the Virgin Islands. *New York Academy of Sciences* 18:463–578.

1987   Whom Did Columbus Discover in the West Indies? *American Archaeology* 6 (2):83–87, www.millersville.edu/~columbus/data/art/ROUSE-01.ART, accessed on February 7, 2008.

1989   Peoples and Cultures of the Saladoid Frontier in the Greater Antilles. In *Early Ceramic Population Lifeways and Adaptive Strategies in the Caribbean*, edited by Peter E. Siegel. British Archaeological Reports, International Series 506.

1992   *The Taínos.* Yale University Press.

Rouse, Irving, and R. E. Alegría.

1990   *Excavations at Maria de la Cruz Cave and Hacienda Grande Village Site, Loíza, Puerto Rico.* Yale University.

Rush, Barbara

1999   *Imperialism, Race, and Resistance: Africa and Britain, 1919–1945.* Routledge.

Sahlins, Marshall

1987   *Islands of History.* University of Chicago Press.

Sanoja, M.

1988   La formación de cazadores recolectores en Venezuela. In *Actas del Segundo Simposio de la Fundación de Arqueología del Caribe.* Washington, D.C.

Sauer, Carl O.

1966   *The Early Spanish Main.* University of California Press.

Saunders, Nicholas J.

2005   *The Peoples of the Caribbean.* ABC-CLIO.

Schell, R. F., and D. M. Musher (editors)

1983   *Pathogenesis and Immunology of Treponemal Infection.* Marcel Dekker.

Schmidt, Peter R.

1997   Archaeological Views on a History of Landscape Change in East Africa. *Journal of African History* 38:393–421.

Schmidt, Peter R., and Thomas C. Patterson (editors)

1996   *Making Alternative Histories: The Practice of Archaeology and History in Non-Western Settings.* School of American Research Press.

Scott, R., A. Oyuela, and P. Carmichael

1991   A Comparison of the Earliest Ceramic Technologies of Ecuador and Colombia. Paper presented at the 56th Annual Meeting of the Society for American Archaeology, New Orleans.

Service, E.

1962   *Primitive Social Organisation: An Evolutionary Perspective.* Random House.

Siegel, Peter

1992   Ideology, Power, and Social Complexity in Prehistoric Puerto Rico. Ph.D. dissertation, Department of Anthropology, State University of New York at Binghamton.

1996   Ideology and Culture Change in Puerto Rico: A View from the Community. *Journal of Field Archaeology* 23:313–33.

Stevens-Arroyo, Antonio M.

1988　*Cave of the Jagua: The Mythological World of the Taínos.* University of New Mexico Press.

Steyn, Maryna, and Maciej Henneberg

1995　Pre-Columbian Presence of Treponemal Disease: A Possible Case from Iron Age Southern Africa. *Current Anthropology* 36 (5):868–73, www.jstor.org/pss/2744035, accessed on February 16, 2008.

Stokes, Anne A., and David Steadman

1999　A Phase I Survey of Marianne Estate, Blanchisseuse, Trinidad. Southeastern Archaeological Research, Inc. Gainesville, Fla.

Sued Badillo, Jalil

1978　*Los Caribes: Realidad o fábula?* Editorial Antillana.

Tabío, E.

1984　Nueva periodización para el studio de las communidades aborígenes de Cuba. *Islas* (Universidad Central de las Villas) (May–Aug.) 78:37–52.

Thomas, David Hurst

1999　*Archaeology: Down to Earth.* Wadsworth Thomson Learning.

Torres, Joshua, and Reniel Rodríguez Ramos

2008　The Caribbean: A Continent Divided by Water. *Archaeology and Geoinformatics: Case Studies from the Caribbean,* edited by Basil A. Reid, pp. 13–29. University of Alabama Press.

Tuzin, D., and Paula Brown (editors)

1983　*The Ethnography of Cannibalism.* Society for Psychological Anthropology.

Vargas, I.

1987　Sociedad y naturaleza: Mediaciones y determinaciones del cambio social. In *Actas del Tercer Simposio de la Fundación de Arqueologia del Caribe.* Taraxacum.

Veloz Maggiolo, M.

1991　*Panorama histórica del Caribe precolombino.* Banco Central, Dominican Republic.

1997　The Daily Life of the Taíno People. In *Taíno: Pre-Columbian Art and Culture from the Caribbean,* edited by Fatima Bercht, Estrellita Brodsky, John Alan Farmer, and Dicey Taylor, pp. 34–45. Monacelli Press.

Veloz Maggiolo, M., E. Ortega, and P. Pina

1974　*El Caimito: Un antiguo complejo ceramista de las Antillas Mayores.* Ediciones Fundación Garcia Arévalo.

Veloz Maggiolo, M., I. Vargas, M. Sanoja, and F. Luna Calderón

1976　*Arqueología de Yuma, República Dominicano.* Taller.

Veloz Maggiolo, M., and B. Vega

1982　The Antillean Preceramic: A New Approximation. *Journal of New World Archaeology* 5:33–44.

Wallerstein, Immanuel

2004　*World-Systems Analysis: An Introduction.* Durham University Press.

Watters, David

1994　Archaeology of Trants, Montserrat. Part 1. Field Methods and Artifact Density Distributions. *Annals of Carnegie Museum* 63:265–95.

Watters, David R., and Richard Scaglion

1994   Beads and Pendants from Trants, Montserrat: Implications for the Pre-
        historic Lapidary Industry in the Caribbean. *Annals of Carnegie Museum*
        63:215–37.

Wenke, Robert J., and Deborah I. Olszewski

2007   *Patterns in Prehistory: Humankind's First 3 Million Years.* Oxford University
        Press.

White, Tim D.

1992   *Prehistoric Cannibalism at Mancos 5Mtumr-2346.* Princeton University Press.

Whitehead, N. L.

1995   Ethnic Plurality and Cultural Continuity in the Native Caribbean: Remarks
        and Uncertainties as to Data and Theory. In *Wolves from the Sea: Readings
        in the Anthropology of the Native Caribbean,* edited by N. L. Whitehead,
        pp. 91–112. KITLV Press.

Williams, D.

1992   El araico en el noroeste de Guyana y los comienzos de la horticultura. In
        Prehistoria sudAmericana: Nuevas perspectivas. Taraxacum.

Wilson, Samuel M.

1990   *Hispaniola: Caribbean Chiefdoms in the Age of Columbus.* University of Ala-
        bama Press.

1997   The Caribbean before European Conquest. In *Taíno: Pre-Columbian Art and
        Culture from the Caribbean,* edited by Fatima Bercht, Estrellita Brodsky, John
        Alan Farmer, and Dicey Taylor, pp. 15–17. El Museo Del Barrio, Monacelli
        Press.

1999   Cultural Pluralism and the Emergence of Complex Societies in Greater An-
        tilles, http://uts.cc.utexas.edu/~swilson/wilson_iaca99.html. Presented at the
        Eighteenth International Congress for Caribbean Archaeology, St. George's,
        Grenada, July, accessed on August 11, 2007.

2007   *The Archaeology of the Caribbean.* Cambridge University Press.

Wolf, Eric

1982   *Europe and the People without History.* University of California Press.

Index